THE
ESSENTIAL
SOCIAL
SKILLS
HANDBOOK
FOR TEENS

THE
ESSENTIAL
SOCIAL
SKILLS
HANDBOOK
FOR TEENS

Fundamental Strategies for Teens and Young Adults
to Improve Self-Confidence, Master Social Anxiety
and Fulfill Their Potential in the 2020s

By **Richard Meadows**

RaiseYouthRight

CONTENTS

EXTRA BONUS

Want to Raise Resilient, Confident, and Future-Ready Teens?

Parenting teens comes with its own set of challenges, but you don't have to navigate it alone. We've created **The Complete Checklist for Raising Resilient, Confident, and Future-Ready Teens**—a practical guide filled with actionable tips from parenting experts, counselors, and teachers to help you support your teen's growth and success.

https://www.raiseyouthright.com/c/checklist

Introduction

I remember my first day of high school. I spent hours choosing just the right outfit and spent hours getting ready. It was high school. I wasn't a kid anymore. This was the big deal. What I'd waited all these years for. Sure, I was nervous. Would I make new friends? Would I fit in? So, I took a deep breath, and off I went. When I arrived, it was loud and busy and people were everywhere...but they all seemed to know exactly where to go and what to do. All of a sudden, I was terrified. All my plans just vanished. And, I felt like I was smothering. Like I somehow didn't belong. That little voice in my head whispered, "You can't do this." All I wanted to do was get away.

Sound familiar? If so, you're not alone. The teen years are some of the hardest years to navigate. Your body is still changing and maturing. Parts of your brain that help with decision-making are still growing. In fact, a teenage brain undergoes a period of zing that can be quite overwhelming for you and your parents. Yeah, there's actually a reason teens do things that make parents scratch their heads. Your brain is still maturing. As a teen, you're between the time of being a kid and being an adult. Add in hormones changing and you've got the recipe for an emotional roller coaster no one is prepared for.

Now, that doesn't mean you can blame bad behavior on your brain. It just means that the part of your brain that is responsible for decision making and being able to see long-term consequences isn't quite done growing yet. So, sometimes, teens do things that grown-ups know will not end well. It leaves grown-ups wondering, "What did you do that for?" You're probably nodding your head because you've had that very conversation with your parents. We all have.

At the same time, your teen years can be some of the most exciting and carefree times you will have in life. You'll be experiencing so many things for the first time. You will be learning so much about yourself, about others, and about the world we live in. You'll be laying the groundwork for the adult you'll become.

While all this is happening, it is normal to experience some highs and lows, struggles and wins. It's a common assumption that all teens are moody and aloof and demanding, wanting to be "grown". There's actually a name for this phenomenon. It's called *teen angst*. It isn't a mental health condition per se, but rather a period when teens are navigating through all of the changes and stressors involved with maturing. Adults sometimes see this as "just being a teenager" and in some ways, yes. That is exactly what is happening. There's more though. *Angst* is a word that means fear, worry, or dread. It stems from feelings of insecurity or apprehension. It's especially evident in teens because, let's be honest, the teen years are a period of intense, rapid growth and change. No one is prepared and we all go through it.

What if it didn't have to be so traumatic and dramatic? What if you could learn to manage your emotions and build a foundation of confidence and strength? Well, I'm here to tell you that you can.

Who Am I?

Hi, I'm Richard Meadows and I was "that" teen. The one who struggled with self-esteem and confidence. The one who wrestled with social anxiety. The one who wanted so desperately to feel ok. I wanted to be able to go places and do things and have that easy-going life I saw so many of my friends living. Did they have their own stressors? Sure. Somehow, mine just felt different. I knew something was different but at the time, I didn't know what it was. I just felt like I somehow didn't fit and trying to just leave me feeling scared and defeated.

The age-old advice of "just deal with it" wasn't helpful.

I don't remember the exact moment, but at some point, I just had enough. I had a choice to make. I could do one of two things:

I could let things stay the same and continue to be a scared, shy, anxious kid who silently wished to be someone else. Or,

I could suck it up and DO something about it.

 I started educating myself on what I was experiencing. I read everything I could find. I sought out counseling to help me understand what was happening. I learned that I was dealing with anxiety and I learned what it really looks like, especially for a teen. It's not all "panic attacks" and being scared to raise my hand in class. It's so much more. It's the feelings of insecurity and isolation. It's the fear of rejection and judgment. It's not feeling confident in myself to speak my mind and not knowing how to say what I feel. It was all that and so much more. The more I learned, the better I started to feel too. I actually tried the strategies I was learning about. And, you know what? Over time, it helped. A lot.

When I was going through my teen years, there weren't a lot of resources written just for teens. Most of the books and resources were for adults. While they helped me, they didn't really speak my language. I wasn't an adult yet so some of the advice just didn't apply. A lot of things helped though, and I can say proudly that I made it to adulthood with a better handle on my anxiety and a better understanding.

As I made my way through my teens and into adulthood, I made it my mission to figure out just what all this anxiety was about and more importantly, what I could do about it. I set out on a journey to healing myself and finding what worked. I wanted to pay it forward. I wanted to give the next generation what wasn't available for me.

And that's how this book was born.

Why This Book and Why Now?

If we all go through these teen struggles and somehow make it to adulthood, you might be wondering, "Well, why this book and why now?" And that's a legit question. Why now?

You've probably heard people say things like:

Kids today have it so easy...

When I was your age...

Back in the day...

You've heard it. Probably a lot. I did too. It's a sentiment that every teen has heard from grown-ups at one time or another, probably from time immemorial. And, like every teen before you, you've probably rolled your eyes and thought, "You don't get it." And know what? You're right. They don't. I don't. But, not for the reasons you might think. Still, it doesn't make being a teen any easier or make the grown-ups in your life totally wrong either. In some ways, you're both right. Let me explain.

The fact is, every generation of teens deals with things the previous generations didn't. For example, when my dad was a teen, there was no TV, no internet, and no cell phones. Seriously. In my teen years, we had cell phones the size of a brick, and cable TV was the coolest thing to have. The Internet was not a thing yet. My parents thought my musical choices were "trash", but then their parents thought the same thing about their "rock and roll".

You are growing up in a time that your parents or grandparents couldn't have imagined. Teens today are faced with a world of real-time information streams, and instant gratification, and social pressures unlike those of previous generations. It's a different kind of pressure and it's increasing. Teens report feeling pressure to be perfect in every area and have it all figured out more than ever before. Social media has only added to that pressure. You are the first generation to navigate social media and have to deal with the realities of an online community. Likes and shares and clicks have become a source of validation and support. Teen depression and anxiety are on the rise. The pressure is intense and has implications for your emotional well-being and self-esteem.

I was that teen and I see what today's teens are struggling with. I found what worked for me and I want to share that with you. There's never been a better time until now.

Why This Book Is Different

Just from my own experience, I found that a lot of books give a ton of vague advice and not a lot of practical stuff you can use. Or they present a lot of complicated techniques and strategies that teens either won't do or need a therapist to help with. Now, don't get me wrong, there are some great resources out there too. I wanted to share some real deal tips and information that was helpful to me and that I used to get myself to a better place and better manage my own anxiety through my teen years. Basically, it's a resource written by someone who has been where you are.

How to Use This Book

The book is divided into chapters, each one addressing some aspects of teen life and coping. We start with focusing on the internal parts of you - your personality, and the roles of self-esteem and confidence. We then move to communication which is a big one for teens and adults alike. Being heard is the key to it all. We then take a closer look at the social factors including social media, social anxiety, and dealing with those situations that are most anxiety-provoking. Finally, we'll explore ways to deal with stress so you can make more time for the fun stuff.

It might surprise you to see that I've included a section just for parents. Let's be real here, your parents are a part of your life and can be a great support. Understanding what you're interested in and trying to accomplish helps them to support you as you learn new ways of dealing with issues. I know, it's hard to imagine your mom or dad was ever your age but, trust me, they were. They may have had different experiences, but the wisdom they have gained is ageless and can help you in your own teen experience.

Finally, you'll find a section with resources that you can use to get help or learn more. I've also included tools and templates that can make organizing your journey just a little easier.

There is no right or wrong way to use this book. It all depends on your style of learning and what you're most comfortable with. You can start at the beginning and read each chapter in order. Or, some people prefer to skim the table of contents and read the chapters that interest them the most first. Either way, the important thing is to read the book. Lots of people buy books and then never actually read them. They then complain that "it didn't help". Well, of course, it didn't if they didn't read it.

We learn by doing.

Throughout each chapter, you'll find questions that are meant to get you thinking about your own situation, experiences, and ways of coping. You'll find information and suggestions for new ways of dealing with what's stressing you. I would suggest keeping a notebook or journal to make notes. I will be asking you to think about some things and sometimes, answer questions. A notebook or journal is a powerful way to keep track of what you're learning and a way to look back as you continue. The very act of writing also helps you to remember and take in what you're learning. Your brain will accept what you give it. If you choose not to keep the notebook, that's ok. This book is not meant to feel like homework. I want this experience to be a good one for you.

At the end of each chapter, you'll find a "Now It's Your Turn" section. Here you'll find a suggested activity or strategy to try based on what was discussed in the chapter. This is where the learning *really* happens.

We learn in two ways. We learn information by reading, listening, and observing. We also learn by experience - by using what we've learned from reading, listening, and observing. The first few (or hundred) times may not go well. That's ok, if you already know how to do something, why would you need to learn? We master skills through trial and error. We try and fail, try and fail until we try and succeed.

Here's an example:

Humans aren't born walking. We have to learn. First, we crawl, then we pull up, and then come to our first steps. You probably don't remember but in the beginning, you toppled over times before you walked on your own. You were trying and failing until you tried and succeeded. The more you did it, the better you got at it. Over time, you mastered walking. And, you were pretty dang proud.

The same idea holds for anything we learn from riding a bike, to learning to write, to playing baseball...even learning things like communicating, coping skills, and managing emotions. It all starts with a try.

Another way you can use this book is with a trusted friend or adult or even a counselor. Sometimes, we can't see our own behavior clearly or as others see it. Having a perspective from outside ourselves can be helpful. Of course, at the end of the day, the decisions you make are your own but having another point of view (not someone telling you what to do) can be helpful. If you're not as confident in yourself as you'd like to be, having someone validate what you're doing or thinking of doing can be helpful.

I hope that you will find not just practical advice here but also some inspiration. You are living in a time of endless possibilities and exciting advances. The future is yours for the taking. It is my hope that this book gives you one more tool to get you where you want to go and have the life you dream of.

Ready to take that first step? Let's go!

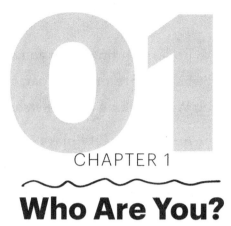

CHAPTER 1

Who Are You?

If I was to ask you, 'Who are you?', you might answer with I'm an athlete, a son, a daughter, a gamer, a musician, or any number of external "roles". And yes, you are those things. However, you are so much more.

Now, if I asked you to describe your personality, what would you say?

Not surprisingly, that's a little bit of a harder question to answer. Because it's kind of complicated.

When it comes to understanding "who you *are*", we are usually talking about who you are on a deeper, more cognitive, and emotional level. We're talking about *personality*.

And, believe it or not, personality plays a pretty big role in not just who you are but how you perceive and navigate the world. It can influence your mood, your self-perception, how you perceive the world, and more.

Since you're reading this book, you are probably seeking to understand yourself better and get some help with navigating through your life with more confidence and just having more fun. Right?

Well, before you can create new skills, you probably want to understand your personality just a bit. For example, I don't like really busy, crowded places. If I am going to work on meeting  new people, doing it at a big crowded event, like a party, is probably going to create more anxiety for me. A smaller setting like coffee with friends, or a smaller, informal gathering might be better for me. Why? Because that's a personality trait I have. It isn't good or bad, right or wrong. It is just me. Can I learn to be in crowded spaces? Sure. And sometime, I might want to. But, while I'm learning new skills, it makes more sense to work with my personality instead of against it.

So, let's look a little deeper at personality and why it matters so much.

What Exactly is Personality?

Personality is a broad construct generally defined as someone's unique patterns of thinking, feeling, and behaving. It's a mix of genetics, your experiences, and your environment, along with your moods, attitudes, and beliefs as well as and opinions. Personality forms early in life and while it can change somewhat over time, your core traits tend to be mostly consistent once you're an adult.

Your personality tends to show when you interact with other people. You might be shy. You might be really talkative. You might tend to be really funny. These are just a few of the many, many characteristics of personality a person could have.

And, just like traits, there are a ton of ways to talk about personality "types". People have been trying to define "personality types" since the Ancient Greeks first identified four basic "temperaments". Now, the Greeks believed that these temperaments were the result of bodily fluids. Eeww. Needless to say, our understanding of personality has come a long way since then.

Even today, there are lots of ways to try and categorize or classify personality types. You've probably heard of some of them. For example, you've probably heard of someone described as a "Type A" personality. You know, that's the driven, rigid, somewhat anxious person.

And, then, there's the Myers-Briggs Type Indicator (MBTI). The MBTI is a popular way of describing personality along four dimensions: focusing outward or inward; attending to sensory information or adding interpretation; deciding by logic or by situation; and making judgments or remaining open.

These are just two of the gazillion ways people try to describe personality. But there is no one single right way.

What the really smart science people have found is that trying to put people in categories doesn't really account for all the ways people differ. For example, you and I can both have anxiety, but the way my anxiety and your anxiety show up can be very different. I might get loud and silly. You might get quiet and walk away.

Without getting too deep into the science-y stuff, what these really smart folks have found is that personality might be better understood based on five basic personality traits. They even have a name for this idea: The Big Five Model.

Basically, each of the Big Five traits focuses on a key aspect of how you think, feel, and act. Here are the Big Five:

BIG 5 TRAITS

EXTROVERSION

Extroversion is the opposite of introversion and is characterized by assertiveness and sociability.

OPENNESS

Openness to experience is characterized by things such as originality, curiosity, and creative imagination.

AGREEABLENESS

Agreeableness is characterized by cooperation, kindness and compassion, respectfulness, and trust.

CONSCIENTIOUSNESS

Conscientiousness includes aspects of organization, reliability, productivity, and responsibility.

NEUROTICISM

Neuroticism is characterized by uneasiness and a tendency towards anxiety and depression.

These are dimensions of personality we ALL have to some degree and there is no one "right" combo. In fact, you can even have differences in the traits themselves. For example, on the agreeableness dimension, you might be super kind to people but not much of a team player. Cooperation might be hard for you and you might tend to struggle with activities where you have to work together. It doesn't mean that's a "bad" trait or a "good trait. It just is part of the overall personality. Traits are important, but your genetics and your experiences also shape your personality. These dimensions are a way to kind of describe your personality.

I am telling you about personality because guess what? Personality has a role in how you experience and react to things, how you learn things, how to think about things.

How would you describe your personality? You don't have to use the words of the Big Five. Just write down some words you might use to describe yourself and your personality. If you get stuck, it's ok to look at the dimensions of the Big Five.

What did you come up with?

Understanding your unique personality will help you as we go along and start talking about new skills and strategies.

You'll like some of them. Others you will probably look at and say, "Nope." And, that's ok. Not every strategy fits every person. Part of that is personality. And that's what makes us all unique. The good news is, there are a gazillion ways to learn how to do something new.

So, now let me tell you why personality matters to what we will be talking about in the following chapters.

Your Teenage Personality – What Happened?

Remember at the beginning of this chapter, I told you that your personality forms early in life? Generally, that's about from infancy to late childhood. Then, an interesting thing happens. As you enter your teens, that process takes a pause.

The teen years are a time of change and growth unlike any you will experience again. Your body, your hormones, and your brain are undergoing crazy amounts of change. And, it's a time of change for your personality too. No, you don't wake up one morning totally different than you were the night before. But, there's something happening. Its kind of like all your personality traits are getting all shaken up and how it all shakes out will help shape your personality and experiences going into adulthood.

Really smart science people have found that during the early to mid-teen years, there are changes in personality that fit with the whole idea of the "moody teen". (You've probably had someone tell you something like that. I know I did.) Anyway, they found that teens tend to become more emotional, less orderly, and lacking self-control, among other things. It kind of sounds like the moody, messy, impulsive teen that grown-ups talk about, huh? Well, now you can tell them that there's a reason! In a nice way of course!

Scientists think that part of the reason for this temporary change in personality has to do with the brain. In your teens, your brain does this cool thing called "pruning". Like pruning the branches of a tree, your brain is cutting back neurons and connections that were  overproduced in early childhood. It sounds bad but it's really a very good thing. It's a normal process that helps to promote brain growth as you mature.

Now, why am I telling you all this? Because a lot of what you learn and experience during this time will help to shape your personality and your adult experiences. Learning how to manage your emotions and learning skills to navigate your world now will help you to transition into adulthood confident and ready to take on the world.

If you stay stuck in those patterns that don't work for you, or choose not to change them, you risk stepping into adulthood without the skills you need.

The good news is that you CAN learn how to manage your emotions and kick social anxiety to the curb. You CAN learn new skills to improve your self-confidence and set yourself up for success.

So, what do you need to know as we get started?

1 If you find your behavior or mood changing, it's not your imagination. It's that thing called adolescence. Know that it might happen. Now, that does NOT mean it's OK to use it as an excuse to be mean or disrespectful. The rules still apply and there are things you can do to check yourself.

2 Even though your brain is doing its thing, you have the power to shape a lot of what will happen going forward. You can help guide your brain to gain the knowledge you need. Every experience you have creates connections

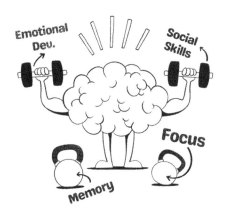

in your brain and stores information. Right now, your brain is like a sponge and it is soaking up all kinds of information.

If there are skills you want to learn, now is the time! Just like the athlete who wants to play better, so they practice...and practice some more.

If you're reading this book, there are skills you're looking to learn, right? Maybe you want to improve your communication skills or overcome your social anxiety. You have to learn the skills you need to do that. You learn them, and practice, and practice some more. Every time you practice and use the skills, you're helping your brain learn and store the info you'll need. Over time, you can be more at ease talking to new people or going to new places. Practice helps the brain grow.

3 Your brain is on GO right now and you have no brakes yet. It's kind of like learning to ride a bike. You're learning and have some balance going but you still need the training wheels. The brain prunes and grows in a certain way and parts of your brain take longer than others.

You've probably heard a lot lately about the adolescent brain not being fully developed until about age 23 or so. It's been all over the news. There is some truth to this and it's one of the reasons that teens tend to make what adults consider bonehead moves.

It turns out that the parts of the brain responsible for good decision-making are among the last to finish growing. So, you're more likely to make decisions that leave adults scratching their heads, and you'll sometimes hear, "You should have known better." Well, maybe but the brain didn't get the message yet.

This is the time of your life when you're having all kinds of new experiences and you want to try new things. The impulsive part of your brain says, "Yeah, let's go!!" It isn't thinking about the possible consequences yet because that part isn't done growing yet. In other words, your brain is telling you to ditch the training wheels, not thinking about the possibility that you'll wreck out. It's just ready to go!

I'm telling you this because it means you need to be on guard for those situations. You don't want to do something you can't take back. Get in the habit of doing a "Stop and Think" before you do something. Listen to that voice in your head. It's your inner voice telling you DANGER AHEAD. We're going to talk more about that voice later because it can be your BFF if you let it.) Have awesome experiences but look before you leap. (Yeah, I sound like my Grandma – she said that a lot and she was always right.)

4 Your brain is open to anything and everything. What you put into it is what you'll get out. This is one of the best times of your life to learn new things. What will those things be? Will you learn the things that you will need to live the healthy, happy, and productive adult life you wish for? Or, will you learn the things that will keep you unhappy and struggling to have the life you want? The cool thing is you can

choose. And, the fact that you chose this book is a sure sign that you're looking to learn the good stuff! Take good care of your brain and it will take good care of you.

So I've told you all this brain and personality stuff because I want you to know that while we are born with what the sci-ence-y folks call genetic predispositions, your experiences and what you do in life have a huge influence on what actually happens. In other words, genes are the foundation but how they are expressed is mostly up to what happens in life. For example, say your mom is super anxious. You may have inherited the tendency to be anxious. Does that mean you will be super anxious too? Nope. It just means that the possibility is there. You can choose to do things to lessen the chance of being super anxious, and maybe not even anxious at all. Cool huh?

So, in the following chapters, we are going to take a look at ways you can learn the skills you need to make the most of your teen years and head into adulthood ready to take on the world.

As we get started, let me ask you this:

What is the thing you want most to get out of this book? What do you most want to learn? What personality traits do you have that you think will help you most? What personality traits do you think you might need to work on? Write it down.

Remember what I said in #2 above about your brain needing some guidance? Writing it down is a way of setting your intention. And, once you write it down, congratulations. You just told your brain, "We're about to learn something so pay attention."

OK, if you're ready, let's go!

CHAPTER 2

Self Esteem, Confidence, And Being Your Best Self

You've probably heard the old saying or some variation of it, "It all starts with you." As cliché as that sounds, it really is true. But what does it really mean, and what does it have to do with being at your best?

The fact is, you don't just wake up one day and do stuff. Everything we do is guided by our experiences and how we interpret them. In other words, how you think, feel and act all starts in your head. You decide what you're going to say or do. The cool part about this is that YOU get to decide. Not your parents. Not your friends. Just you.

Going back to that first day of school I told you about, I felt so out of place. I felt like everyone I saw had it all together. In my head, all I could hear was, "You can't do this." And, at that moment, I believed it. It took me a while to figure out why I told myself those things and that my anxiety was a liar.

When it comes to being at your best and living the life you want, it all starts with how you think and feel about yourself. It's the things you tell yourself about you that shape how you navigate your world. Are you confident in yourself and who you are? Do you value yourself?

So, let's take a closer look and how all this fits together.

What Is Self-Esteem?

Self-Esteem is essentially your opinion of yourself – how you feel about everything about yourself – your strengths (yes we all have them), your abilities, and even your weak areas (we all have those too). It is a set of core beliefs that we have about ourselves. When you have healthy self-esteem, you feel good about yourself and feel deserving of respect from yourself and others.

People with healthy self-esteem:

◇ Believe in themselves and feel good about themselves

◇ Feel liked and accepted by others

◇ Feel proud of what they do

◇ Respect themselves and feel deserving of respect from others

People with low self-esteem:

◇ Feel undeserving of respect

◇ Feel bad about themselves

◇ Judge themselves harshly

◇ Don't feel good/ worthy enough

When you have low self-esteem, you don't feel good about yourself or deserving of respect and kindness.

Self-esteem isn't just something that shows up. It develops over time through our experiences and our own ways of processing.

Interactions With Others

The people in your life can affect how you feel about yourself. Sometimes people are patient and kind and positive. When the focus is on what's good about us, we feel good about ourselves. When they are patient when we make mistakes, we learn to accept ourselves. When we have friends and get along, we feel liked, valued, and accepted by others.

Sometimes, though, the people in our lives are not as kind or patient as we would like them to be. Whoever said, "sticks and stones can break my bones, but words will never harm me" was wrong. Harsh or hurtful words can and do hurt, even if the hurt doesn't show on the outside. Those words can stick with you, and affect how you think about yourself. For example, if parents or teachers scold or harshly criticize more than they praise, it can be hard to feel good about you. Bullying from siblings or other kids can hurt your self-esteem, too.

What You Tell Yourself - That Inner Voice

Every person has thoughts and feelings about themselves. And, everyone has what's commonly referred to as an "inner voice" or "inner dialogue" that echoes what we think about ourselves. Seriously. Everyone has one.

One time, someone who was trying to help me asked me about my inner voice. The first thing I said was, "No dude, that's crazy. I don't hear voices." Now, before you decide, hey that's crazy, hear me out.

Having an inner voice or dialogue is not the same as hearing voices. Your inner voice, or inner dialogue, is nothing more than your thoughts. It's that little voice that comments on everything happening in your life, and even what you're thinking about. Sometimes you're aware of that inner voice, sometimes you're not. Either way, that dialogue is running nonstop. It's always there, and it's always listening, waiting to comment.

The reason we're talking about this inner voice or "self-talk" is because it forms the foundation for how you feel about yourself. And, how you feel about yourself affects your self-esteem, your confidence, and your sense of well-being.

Think about this: Have you ever stopped and listened to what you tell yourself? How many times have you found yourself thinking, "I'm such a loser." "I can't do anything right." "No one is going to like me." Thoughts like that feed a negative sense of self-worth and your anxiety tells you it's true, even when it's not.

Low self-esteem is a thinking problem. When you speak to yourself or view yourself in a negative way, you start to believe that's who you are. If your brain hears "I'm a loser" long enough, it starts to believe it. And it doesn't end there.

Without getting too science-y on you, there's a phenomenon called the confirmation bias. Confirmation bias is the tendency to seek out and place importance on information that confirms the beliefs you have, even when there is evidence that it's not true. You simply place more weight on those bits of information that validate what you think, interpret it as evidence, and act as if it's true. You'll see this bias at its strongest with highly emotional issues or deeply held beliefs. And, because the brain believes what we tell it, it's taken as fact and becomes the basis for actions.

Here's an example: Say, your inner voice is constantly saying, "You never do anything right. Why do you keep trying? You'll just embarrass yourself." Looking for evidence, you may focus on the fact that while playing basketball with your friends, you missed a shot. Under normal circumstances, that would be frustrating but not the be all and end all. For someone struggling with a nasty inner critic, that one miss is "EVIDENCE" that they're not good at anything. Everyone was laughing at you. The result? Hear that criticism long enough and people stop trying. What it looks like on the outside can be isolation, avoiding time with friends, or not playing a sport you otherwise would enjoy.

When Thoughts Turn Negative

As you can see, our thoughts play a very important role in determining how we feel. Of course, we all have upsetting thoughts about ourselves sometimes. They can be about the past, the present, or even the future. These thoughts are powerful and can be quite harsh.

Imagine hearing this 24/7. After a while, you start to believe it. And, over time, you start to behave as if it were always true. Now, here's the thing, those harsh, negative thoughts you have about yourself are NOT 100% true all the time. Sometimes they are. Other times, they're partly true, and sometimes, a lot of times, they are not true at all. The problem comes when you assume they're always true.

Have you ever really listened to what you say to yourself? What are some of the negative things your inner voice says to you on the regular? Are they kind? Or are they harsh and hurtful?

Here's the 411: There is nothing wrong with you. Are you perfect or an expert at every single thing? Of course not. No one is. You're human. You make mistakes. And, welcome to the real world - we are ALL imperfect.

And, here's something else to keep in mind: these negative thought patterns are also a key player in social anxiety. We will be talking more about that in a later chapter but just know that getting those negative ways of thinking in check can help you in so many areas of your life and well-being.

One of the keys to building a stronger sense of self-esteem is creating a more positive way of thinking about yourself. That sense of self also feeds your belief in yourself and your confidence. If you don't feel good about yourself, you are surely not going to put yourself out there.

Self-Confidence: What is It?

Self-confidence is one of those broad terms that can be hard to define exactly but you know it when you see it. Being self-confident means that you have faith and trust in your abilities. You accept who you are and feel a sense of control in your life. When you're self-confident, you feel able to handle situations, even hard ones.

Have you ever met someone that just seems to be able to handle whatever comes along? Or someone who always seems to say or do just the right thing at the right time? It might be tempting to think they are just "lucky" in some way. I promise you, it didn't just fall into their laps. Everyone is different and deals with different things.

So where does self-confidence come from?

Self-confidence, like self-esteem, is mostly formed by our early learning experiences and influence from important people in our lives like parents, teachers, siblings, and peers. Kids who are encouraged to be independent and allowed to solve problems tend to feel successful and more positive about their abilities. Kids who didn't have those opportunities or struggled with learning those skills tend to feel less confident in their abilities.

Friends can affect your confidence too. And as you get older, friends can really influence how you think and feel about yourself. Let's be real - we care about what our friends think. Sometimes, those expectations are ridiculously high or even unrealistic. You can get caught up in trying to be who you think you should be or do what you think you should do. When you try and try but can't reach that ridiculously high bar, confidence crumbles.

Even your unique personality traits and characteristics play a part sometimes. Some people just seem to have traits that help them deal with things more easily.

Regardless of how it forms or what the influences are, you need to remember this: self-confidence is not a reflection of your abilities or strengths. It is about your **belief** in your abilities.

Some days, you're going to feel like a superhero, that you can take on the world and win. Other days, you may feel

totally defeated. That's normal. Self-confidence isn't a straight line. There are just some days when you wonder if you have what it takes to be successful. When a lack of confidence starts to hold you back, then Houston, we've got a problem.

What does low self-confidence look like? It's sneaky. It quietly shows up as negativity, self-doubt, and fear. Fear convinces you that you can't do what you want. Fear keeps you from putting yourself out there. It stops you dead in your tracks and keeps you stuck.

But what we know is that confidence and self-esteem don't just happen. They are nurtured over time. Sometimes we aren't even aware of it. Our experiences, our internal thoughts, and feelings, our interactions with others all help to contribute to how we feel about ourselves.

And the good news? You can build a healthy sense of confidence and self-esteem!

Like self-esteem, self-confidence is very much a thinking problem based on unrealistic thoughts and feelings that hold you back. The good news is, it doesn't have to stay that way. Change how you *think* and you can change your life.

Building self-confidence means overcoming that fear and learning to believe in yourself and your abilities. It's time to get unstuck, my friend.

Building a More Confident You

First up - Self-esteem because everything starts with how you think about yourself as a person. Remember, I said that low self-esteem is a thinking problem. Those negative beliefs convince us that we can't be successful, that we are undeserving and somehow less than. We assume the worst and expect the worst. As a result, we start to avoid the people and places and things that we love. Over time, all these negative feelings and all this avoidance increases your anxiety and doubts which only makes those negative thoughts all that much more believable. Remember when I said your anxiety is a liar? Yeah, it convinces you to be afraid and avoid the very things that could help you.

So what can you do about all this negative thinking and self-talk? You challenge it. Remember we said that low self-esteem is a thinking problem and that our core thoughts and beliefs are assumptions, not fact? Assumptions can be changed. You have to challenge how you think to change how you think.

Silence Your Inner Critic

"I can achieve anything I want"

"I deserve love and kindness"

"I am enough"

"No one likes me"

"Can't do anything right"

"Loser"

Would you talk to your best friend like that? Um, no. So, ask yourself, why. Why would you talk to yourself like that?

When you feel those negative thoughts creeping in, you have to challenge them.

TRY THIS

Make a list of the things your inner critic likes to tell you. Now think of things that contradict what's on your list. For example, if your inner critic likes to say, "You are always wrong", think about times when you've been right about something. Write down lots of examples. While this seems like such a simple task, you're giving your brain something positive to focus on: "That's not true. I am right about a lot of things and here's the proof."

The more you can challenge those negative thoughts and replace them with positive ones, the healthier your sense of self becomes. Over time, you'll be able to recognize when your inner voice is being nasty and say "Hey, knock it off." You'll be able to shift to a more positive inner dialogue and self-talk. Speaking kindly to yourself will become a habit for you.

Now that's powerful stuff. Now let's look at the other side of self-esteem.

Self-Confidence: Get Some!

To overcome a lack of confidence, you have to redefine how you think about yourself and your abilities. You can do that by basically restructuring how you think about things and the choices you make. That restructuring happens by doing things that let you experience success and build trust in yourself.

Focus On Your Strengths

We all have things we are really good at. It's important to know what skills and abilities you have that you can rely on. What are your strengths? What are those things about you that just come naturally or that you're just really good at?

Do more of those things! For example, if you draw well, keep doing it. If you're a wicked good ballplayer, keep it up. Maybe you're just a really cool big brother or big sister to your siblings or like to volunteer at the animal shelter. Whatever that strength is, express your own style in ways that reflect who you genuinely are. Likewise, if you have a special talent or interest, take the time to nurture it. Focusing on your strengths reinforces your sense of confidence and accomplishment.

Plan for Success

When you are prepared for something, you naturally feel more confident. This can be especially true when faced with a situation that is stressful or anxiety-provoking. Knowing that you have a plan you can rely on going in alleviates some of the fear and allows your confidence and courage to come through. Yes, courage. When fear is moved aside, it is courage that comes forward.

One Step At A Time

Confidence comes from taking action. Your plan gives you a roadmap for success. When making the plan, it's important to break your task or goal down into small, manageable action steps. Making the steps too big can be overwhelming and, chances are, you won't do it.

Identify your steps and take the first step no matter how small it is. Where you start is up to you and will depend on the goal. The most important thing is to take the first step. Each step reinforces the "yes I can" attitude and the way you think about yourself. One step leads to another…and another.

As If!

Have you ever heard the saying, "Fake it till you make it?" It doesn't mean you're fake. It means that you are going to do something and act "as if" you can already do something. It's actually a proven strategy for change. Basically, it is the idea that you can create the circumstances you want by acting as if they are already true.

For example, you can change how you feel just by smiling. Seriously. Smiling, even when you don't feel like it, increases feelings of happiness.

The same can be applied to your confidence. Acting like someone who is successful and confident can help you to think about yourself in that way too. Remember, I said that your brain believes what you tell it? Well, when you act "as if" your brain begins to restructure those beliefs and expectations you have and strengthen your faith in your abilities.

So how can you do this "as if" thing? A great way is to find a role model. One way to do this is to find a role model. Think of someone who has the kind of confidence you desire. It might be a friend or a sibling. What are this person's actions that convey confidence to you? Try some of those actions for yourself and see how it feels.

If that sounds too weird for you, try this: be an observer. Watch people who appear confident in ways that are meaningful to you. They might be friends, family, or even a celeb you admire. What are they doing that creates the impression of confidence for you? Imagine yourself behaving in a similar way. How could these qualities help you in moving forward towards your goal?

Talk To Yourself

We talked about self-talk in the self-esteem section but it applies here too. Let's be real, how can you feel confident when you have negativity looping over and over in your head? Negative assumptions and self-talk convince you that you can't be successful.

Take a minute and think about what you say to yourself. Is it positive and helpful or is it negative and critical? If it's not positive, it's time to change that thinking!

When you find yourself thinking negatively about yourself, challenge yourself! Stop and take a minute to remind yourself of your strengths. Say something that you're grateful for today.

Try a daily affirmation. OK, yeah, it sounds kind of weird to talk to yourself but it is powerful stuff. Each day remind your-

self of a strength or talent or another positive accomplishment. You can even write it down if it helps you to remember. Some people like to keep their thoughts in a journal. Totally up to you how you do it. The important thing is to do it.

Practice Makes Progress

Like planning, mentally preparing can boost confidence too. You've probably heard of athletes using things like meditation or visualization to prepare for their game. Why? Because it works. Rehearsing or visualizing yourself doing something successfully creates a mental imprint and a feeling of familiarity. When the time comes for the actual event, your brain is likely to respond confidently as if you've already been there and done that.

Say you want to ask someone to HOCO but you're scared. You worry you'll say or do the wrong thing. What if you practiced that whole scene in your head a few times? What would you say or do? How do you imagine it will go? The more you can rehearse in your head, the more comfortable you'll be when the time comes to ask that question.

So now you have some ideas for building that confidence. Where do you want it to take you?

Now It's Your Turn

One of the ways we build confidence and self-esteem is by doing, by trying something new. To grow, we have to step out of our comfort zone because nothing grows there. I know that sounds lame but it's true. If you stay where you are, you never know where you could go. So, it's time to step out of that comfort zone just a tiny bit.

Do something you've never done before.

Think of something you've wanted to do but have not because you felt inadequate or not confident in your ability. It doesn't have to be anything crazy. It does have to be a safe activity. No risky behavior. It should be something that you really want to do but feel afraid of taking the chance. It might be going someplace you've wanted to go. It might be trying out for a part in the school play or singing karaoke. It might be taking your driving test. (This one is a big one for lots of teens who just feel scared and put it off.) It might be making it a point to smile and say hello to someone. Or saying "yes" to an invitation to see a movie with friends. It's up to you what you choose. Only you know where your level of comfort and readiness are.

- What are you choosing to do?
- What are your feelings going into this choice?
- What can you do to prepare for this choice?
- Is your inner critic trying to discourage you?
- How can you challenge your inner critic?
- Following the experience, think about what went well.
- How did that feel to have a positive experience.
- If there were some things that didn't go so well, that's ok.
- Remember nothing and none are perfect

Each time you try something new and experience that bit of success, it FEELS good. That feeling does all kinds of things in your brain that makes you want to do more. Basically, when you accomplish something, especially when it's something you thought you couldn't do, your brain all of a sudden says, "YES! Now, what else can I do?" Success breeds success.

WHAT ARE YOU GOING TO DO?

Before Doing It.

What are your feelings going into this choice?
What can you do to prepare for this choice?
Is your inner critic trying to discourage you?
How can you challenge your inner critic?

Following the experience.

Following the experience, think about what went well.
How did that feel to have a positive experience.
If there were some things that didn't go so well, that's ok.
Remember nothing and none are perfect

CHAPTER 3

Communication

"I didn't say that."

"That's not what I meant."

"You just don't understand."

"You don't listen."

"People aren't interested in what I have to say."

"I never know what to say."

S ound familiar? If so, you're not alone. Expressing yourself is one of the most crucial skills to have and honestly, one of the hardest to master. And, if you think it's only kids who struggle, think again. Of all the critical skills people need in life, communication is the one they struggle with the most. Grown-ups struggle too and when you get a teen and an adult both struggling to communicate, the result is usually frustration, anger, and a whole lot of hurt feelings.

You'd think communicating would be easy. After all, as humans, we learn how to speak pretty early in life. We first learn words from those around us – parents, grandparents, older siblings, and teachers. We learn to speak. Later, we learn more about communicating with others as our social world expands. Friends, siblings, peers, teachers, and even random interactions with others all influence how we communicate. And therein lies part of the problem. Not everyone is a good communicator. We don't always have good communication role models. Not every experience is a positive one. For example, if feelings aren't something talked about much in your family, saying how you feel might be really hard.

Over time, we develop patterns (habits) of communicating. Sure, we learn words but we don't always learn *HOW* to communicate well – how to get your point across, how to express your feelings in healthy ways, how to ask for or accept help and support, love or comfort.

Communication is the foundation of any interaction and relationship. Done well, you each come away feeling heard and respected, maybe even connected. Done poorly, you both come away feeling frustrated and rejected and alone.

Can you imagine if no one ever learned how to communicate? Businesses wouldn't be able to run. Families would disintegrate. Friendships couldn't form. Relationships wouldn't flourish. You wouldn't be able to ask that someone special out or get help with that math homework. Heck, you couldn't even order a burger, hold the onions. Communication is literally a skill that we need and use every single day. How well we use it determines how our interactions with others go.

So, let's take a deep dive into this thing called communication because once you get it, you'll wonder why no one ever told you about it before now. (That's a whole other story. No one kept it from you. It's just something we all take for granted and assume it works...till it doesn't.)

What is Communication?

Easy enough question, right? You probably said, "Duh, it's talking." And, technically, you'd be right. Part of communication is using speech and language. But what if I told you that the talking part is only a tiny piece of communicating?

Yup, there's more to it. A whole lot more.

Communication is the act of sending information from one person (or group) to another. In its simplest form, there is a sender (you), the message, and the recipient, or person you're trying to communicate with. Sounds simple enough, right?

Well, here's where things get complicated. Communication is also more than just words. *How* you send those messages also affects communication.

Verbal communication, or the words, is only a small part of the communication process. In fact, it is estimated that at least 50% (maybe more) of our communication comes from non-verbal messages.

Those non-verbal messages come in the form of:

■ Voice tone (how your voice sounds - is it harsh, sarcastic, soft?)

■ Body language (how you stand or sit, where you put your arms, posture, etc)

■ Facial expressions

■ Gestures (that eye roll, hand gesturing, etc.)

Think about it this way: if you're talking to someone and they're glaring at you, arms crossed, they're sending you a message without saying a word. How would you read that message? Chances are, you would probably assume they're mad and not likely to be in a talkative mood. Communication blocked.

One of the most notorious of these expressions is the infamous eye roll. Who hasn't heard, "Don't you roll your eyes at me." Yeah, we've all done it and honestly, it gets you nowhere good. The eyes tell on us every time.

NON-VERBAL MESSAGES

VOICE TONE

What it sounds like:
How your voice sounds can say a lot!
Is it harsh, sarcastic, or soft?
Imagine saying "I'm fine" in different tones.
How does each one change the meaning?

BODY LANGUAGE

What you do:
Your body talks too! How you stand or sit, where you put your arms, and your posture all send messages. Standing tall shows confidence, slouching might show you're bored or tired.

FACIAL EXPRESSIONS

Show it on your face:
Your face can say it all. A smile can mean you're happy or friendly, while a frown can show you're upset. Raise an eyebrow? That can mean you're curious or skeptical.

GESTURES

Move it:
Even small movements matter.
That eye roll? It can show you're annoyed.
Hand gestures can emphasize your point or show excitement. Just be mindful of what your gestures are saying!

Did you know that eye contact is one of the most powerful influences of communication? It's true. Making eye contact (not rolling your eyes or giving someone a death stare) is a powerful way to let someone know that you are present and interested in what they're saying. More about that later but for now, know that how you present yourself, that non-verbal communication, matters.

Why Is Communicating So Hard?

Communicating is hard for lots of reasons, especially between teens and grown-ups.

Sometimes it's because of differing views but a lot of the time, it's because there's an information traffic jam.

Communication between people is like a highway. There's traffic coming towards you when someone is trying to send information, or communicate, with you. There's traffic going towards the other person when you're trying to send information, or communicate, with them. All along the way, you each have to listen, hear, interpret, and decide how to respond. Just like in a roadway, it's rarely a straight shot. There are twists and turns, curves, bumps, and sometimes, even roadblocks.

Notice that I said "listen" and "hear". You might be thinking, "Wait, those are the same thing." Actually, they're not.

Hearing is the act of taking in and processing sound. There's a specific part of your brain that interprets incoming sounds. Bees buzzing is hearing. A clock ticking is hearing. Your mom's voice telling you to pick your dirty clothes up off the floor is hearing.

Listening is how you interpret that sound. Listening is where we take in the sounds, process them, and apply meaning to them. How well or accurately you accomplish listening is up to you and how you listen to someone.

One thing we know is that there are different ways of listening. We listen to respond or we listen to understand. And which one you choose makes a huge difference.

Here's a real-life example:

Have you ever stood there listening to your mom or dad asking you about something you did or didn't do, like homework or grades? As you hear them speaking, chances are, you're already in your head planning a response. It goes something like this:

Parent: Michael, why didn't you do your homework before you sat down to watch the game? You know we expect homework to be done first.

Michael: Yeah, but it was starting and I didn't want to miss it.

Parent: But you're supposed to have it done before. You should have...

> *Michael: But I didn't want to miss it and what's the big deal. I did part...*
>
> *Parent: Finish...*
>
> *Michael: This is ridiculous (and storms off)*

Now, what happened here? Yes, Michael wanted to watch the game. Yes, he should have finished his homework.  But what the parent never learned was that Michael's bus was late and he did almost all of his homework on the bus so that he'd make it in time for the game. He never got a chance to say that. What Michel never learned was that his parent was about to say, "Finish it at half-time." Instead, the conversation descended into a big mess. Neither Michael nor his parent listened or allowed the other to finish. They were both determined to be the one to respond first, assuming what the other would say, without even knowing all the facts. What could have been a win-win for both of them, turned into an epic fail all around.

Does this scenario sound familiar? It's a scene played out thousands of times a day. And it is not unique to teens and their parents. The fact is, people, tend to listen not to understand but simply to respond. They need to be first, to be right, and usually, they miss a whole lot of info that could have made the situation work out instead of blowing up.

COMMUNICATION   **59**

What if the scenario had gone this way:

> *Parent: Michael, why didn't you do your homework before you sat down to watch the game? You know we expect homework to be done first.*
>
> *Michael: Yeah, but it was starting and I didn't want to miss it. Could I do it at halftime just this once?*
>
> *Parent: I hear you. Yes, do it at halftime please.*
>
> *Michael: OK, I will.*
>
> *Parent: When you're finished, let me know please. Is it a good game?*
>
> *Michael: Really good. Thanks for letting me watch it. I'll come to tell you when I'm done.*
>
> *Parent: You're welcome. Thank you for getting your homework done.*

See the difference? They did 3 things really well:

- They let each other finish their thoughts and didn't interrupt.

- They each acknowledged that they heard the other one and understood. "OK, I hear you", "OK I will."

- They were respectful and said thank you.

It might sound weird for kids and parents to say thank you to each other but think about it. You would say thank you to a friend or even a stranger who did something nice for you or was kind to you, right? Why wouldn't you do that for the people who love you and you love the most?

A key takeaway from this exchange was that in the second one, they *listened* before responding and both of them *got what they needed*. One of the things we know is that sometimes, as we're listening, our brains are already forming a response.

Think about it. How many times have you gotten into a discussion with your mom or dad, you're not liking what you're hearing, and before they've even finished speaking, you've already had a whole convo in your head. They're barely finished and out comes, "Yeah but..." and off you go. Now to be fair, everybody does it sometimes even though it doesn't do anything to help the conversation.

Here's another example. Say you want to ask a friend to borrow a video game. Your friend responds, "Well, I don't know..." and before they can even finish, your brain decides your friend was saying no. You respond with, "Nevermind!" in your best mad voice. Now your friend is mad, you're mad, and it never occurred to you that your friend was trying to say, "I don't know if I can do it now. I will bring it over later." Uh oh.

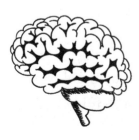

While that's an admirable initiative by your brain, sometimes the brain gets ahead of itself and starts blurting out responses before you've even had a chance to fully take in what's being conveyed to you. Communication stops and no one is hearing or being heard. That's what happens when you listen to just respond and not to understand what the other person's trying to tell you. Part of becoming an effective communicator is learning to listen to understand what is being shared.

Honestly, when it comes to communication, we mostly suck. That is until we learn how. Once you learn how you're going to find that people hear and understand you more clearly, and, you will be able to find the words to express yourself confidently.

What Makes a Good Communicator?

Being a good communicator isn't something you're born with. If we were born good communicators, you and your parents would never argue (can you imagine??). You and your siblings would be BFFs all the time. You and your boyfriend or girlfriend would never have a conflict. You'd be able to say what you want, what you need, and how you feel, AND people would get it. Every. Single. Time.

But, life doesn't work that way. Life is about learning. And just like any other life skill, good communication is something you learn. Once you learn how you'll find that people understand you better and you will feel more confident and respected. You will feel *heard*.

A Good Communicator

Understands the Audience:

Knows who they're talking to. You wouldn't talk to your mom the same way you talk to your friends.

Chooses the Best Medium:

Decides whether to communicate face-to-face, in writing, or by text/email, depending on the situation. Bad news? Always face-to-face.

Selects Appropriate Dialogue:

Creates a safe environment for conversation. Avoid starting defensively to ensure the other person feels comfortable engaging.

Speaks Clearly:

Ensures the message is understood. Be explicit because the other person can't read your mind.

Listens to Understand:

Focuses on truly understanding the other person's message, not just hearing the words.

Asks for Feedback:

Checks for understanding by asking, "Do you get what I'm saying?" to clarify any misunderstandings.

Becoming A Good Communicator

Learning to communicate clearly and effectively takes practice. I won't lie, it can be hard at first. After all, you're undoing a lifetime of doing things a certain way and learning how to use your words and your skills in a whole new way. It can feel weird for sure. You might feel like everyone is looking at you or wondering what the heck you're doing. Honestly, they might be. And that's ok. Whenever someone does something unexpected or new, it gets attention. But it is good attention because half the battle is getting someone's attention in the right way. It's ok to feel a little self-conscious or out of place as you're learning these new ways of communicating.

I'm telling you that because we think learning is just reading a book, like you're doing right now, and somehow new skills just magically appear. Well, I wish that were true but there's no magic to learning. We actually learn by doing. And here's the REALLY important part I want you to hear: part of the learning is failing. Why am I telling you that? Because the fact is, we learn by doing, by failing and succeeding, or by trial and error. Each time we try, we might not get to the goal, but we get a step closer because we are trying to use the new skill, and when we fall short, we can see what worked and what didn't.

Think about it this way: when you were learning how to walk, I guarantee you fell down a hundred times before you even managed that first step. And, yeah, people were watching but you tried again. You fell a bunch more. (Don't believe me? Ask your mom or dad, they might have even captured it on video.) But over time, you added a few steps in between those falls until you figured it out. The point is, the learning comes through doing it over and over till you get it.

One other thing I want you to know – and it's something I wish someone had told me: the doing part may take you waaay out of your comfort zone. It might even make you feel a little anxious at first. That's ok. A little anxiety can be motivating and prompt us to do something, even if we don't want to. It's the same kind of anxiety that made our ancestors learn to run when the dinosaurs showed up. (As we go along, I will share with you some of the things that helped me to be less anxious as I was learning.)

I'm going to share with you some of the best things that helped me when I was learning how to communicate better. I wanted to be able to talk to people without struggling or feeling like no one understood. I wanted to be able to talk to my parents without having an argument. I wanted to be able to ask someone out on a date without feeling like a goof. I wanted to be able to talk to people at ball games and parties and dances and all those places I went with my friends and not feel like I was on the outside looking in.

You Gotta Have Mad Skills

If you're going to communicate well, you need skills.

Active listening

Active listening sounds easy, but it takes work. It's more than just hearing someone speak. When you're actively listening, you are engaged and fully focused on what the person is saying. They have your full attention. Being focused on what someone is saying to you is the most important part of listening.

Let's be honest, it's hard to stay focused. You can be distracted by so many things:

- Daydreaming

- Rehearsing (already thinking of a response)

- Judging the person

- Distractions (looking at your phone, not taking your earbuds out)

What are the things that make it hard for you to actively listen? Think about some ways to minimize their influence.

One of the hardest things for me was to learn to stop looking at my phone. I convinced myself I could listen and peek at the screen at the same time. Was I wrong! The fact is, your brain can only focus on one thing at a time. We like to think we can focus on lots of things but we really can't. We can switch focus or halfway pay attention but we miss a lot when we do that. I'd find myself only hearing half of what someone said and feeling too embarrassed to ask them to repeat it. Needless to say, I eventually learned to put my phone in my pocket.

So just what does active listening look like? How do you know when you're doing it?

ACTIVE LISTENING

It is neutral and non-judgmental (beware of using words like "always" or "never")

It requires patience. In other words, it allows time for people to respond. Don't interrupt. Let there be moments of silence. It's not a bad thing.

It includes both verbal and non-verbal cues that indicate listening (smiling, eye contact, leaning in)

You ask for clarification when you need it. "Am I understanding you correctly?" "I think you mean... is that right?"

You reflect back on what is said. "I hear you saying that you feel sad when I leave for school."

You ask questions. "Can you tell me about that?"

You summarize what someone is saying to be sure you understand. "I think I heard you say that you feel hurt" "I think you mean..."

The silence thing is something that almost everybody struggles with. Silence is just uncomfortable. But it is also a time when you or the other person can use it to reflect, or even take a breath. This breather can be really helpful when tempers are flaring. You do not want to just spit out the first thing that comes into your head. I promise you, it won't be nice and you probably won't get what you want or need. Stop, breathe, and use that moment of silence to get your head together. It lets the other person do the same. There's a lot happening in that silence. Give each other time to reflect and respond. You don't have to fill the silence with chatter.

OK, yeah, you're thinking that is just too much. Honestly, in the beginning, it seems that way. In fact, you are probably doing some of these things already and don't even know it.

The next time you're talking to someone, pay attention to what you're doing. Are you paying attention to what they're saying? Are you trying to understand? What's going on with your body language?

Non- Verbal Communication

Communication is more than words. People communicate information through things like eye contact, gestures, posture, body movements, and tone of voice.

Here's an example: Most kids know "the look". You know, it's the one that will stop you mid-step because you KNOW mom or dad means business. Not a word is spoken yet everything is said at that moment.

There's a funny scene in the Will Ferrell movie, *Talladega Nights*, where Ricky Bobby is being interviewed and his hands are moving in weird ways. He's trying to answer questions and says, "I don't know what to do with my hands." I always think of that scene when trying to explain the importance of body awareness when you're communicating. If you're fidgeting or moving in odd ways, you'll be distracted and the person you're talking to will as well. Communication roadblock. Body language at work.

Verbal and nonverbal communication work together to get your message across. So, it's important that your words and your body language match. Otherwise, your message might get lost like Ricky Bobby's did. especially useful when making presentations or when speaking to a large group of people.

The way you hold your body and your posture, even your facial expressions and gestures convey powerful messages. Communication experts sometimes describe body language as "opened" or "closed". What that means is, your body language can communicate whether you're open and approachable or closed off and not wanting to interact.

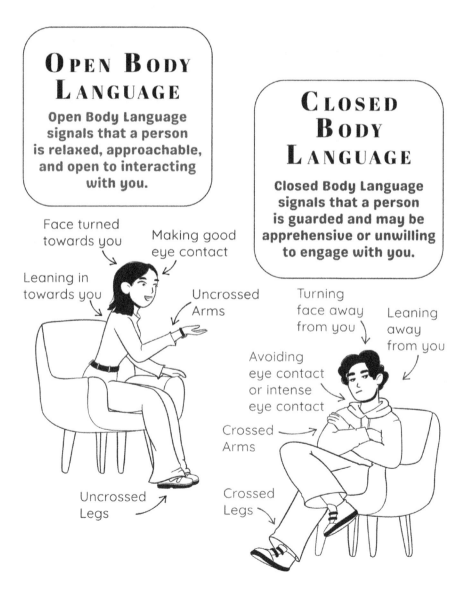

OPEN BODY LANGUAGE

Open Body Language signals that a person is relaxed, approachable, and open to interacting with you.

CLOSED BODY LANGUAGE

Closed Body Language signals that a person is guarded and may be apprehensive or unwilling to engage with you.

Face turned towards you

Making good eye contact

Leaning in towards you

Uncrossed Arms

Uncrossed Legs

Turning face away from you

Leaning away from you

Avoiding eye contact or intense eye contact

Crossed Arms

Crossed Legs

Being closed doesn't always mean that someone doesn't want to engage because they're hostile or upset or don't like you for some reason. Sometimes, people close off out of a need to protect themselves. They don't always know they're doing it. For example, someone who struggles with social anxiety or shyness might unknowingly sit or act in a way that feels protective and keeps people from getting too close. Unfortunately, the other person doesn't always know why someone is closed off. That's when being compassionate and looking for other clues can be helpful.

Do they look scared or nervous?

Do they look like they're feeling alone?

You know, it's ok to ask. You never know when someone could use a friendly helping hand.

Have you ever thought about what *your* body language says? Think about how you sit when you're around other people. Are you relaxed or are your arms crossed or in your pockets? If you're a hoodie fan, where's that hood? Covering your head? If you saw you, what would you think your body language says?

The next time you're having a conversation with your mom or dad and it's kind of headed south, stop and take a quick scan of your body language. How are you standing? Are you looking at them when they speak? What about that voice tone? Are you being sarcastic, maybe not even realizing? If you find yourself being closed off, try changing that body language.

TRY THIS

A cool thing happens when we do something different, especially when others don't expect it. It causes the other person to react differently. This can be the difference between a conversation that goes south and one that at least ends without a battle.

Here's what I mean: Say you and your sister are arguing. Your face is angry, and your voice is getting loud. Your arms are crossed hard. Your sister is angry too and her voice is getting loud too. You know where this is headed right? What if, you just stopped? What if, instead of yelling, you dropped your voice to above a whisper and dropped your hands to your sides. Guess what's likely to happen? Chances are, she's going to stop yelling too. Why? Because it takes two to argue and she's going to look real funny yelling all by herself.

Sometimes, all it takes to improve communication is doing something different that opens the lines of communication instead of blocking them.

Here are a few more tips for improving your communication skills.

Use "I statements." These statements sound silly but they are a powerful way to learn how to express yourself in a way that avoids things like blaming or accusing someone of purposely trying to hurt you.

We tend to use language that is focused on the other person:

"You made me so mad."

"You always laugh at me."

These "You" statements tend to blame or shame the other person. They don't do anything to help you tell someone what you want or need. And, as soon as the accusations fly, no one is listening anymore. Am I right?

A better choice is to express yourself in a way that avoids blaming and shaming and lets the other person know what you want or need. "I statements" do just that. They sound weird but they are POWERFUL.

I-statements are a way of expressing your feelings in a positive way and what you want the other person to know. And they're not hard to use.

"I feel..."

"I need..."

When you begin with 'I', rather than 'You', you are giving the other person information without them feeling attacked.

Can you think of some times you've used "You" statements with others? What "You" statements do you tend to use? Who are you most likely to use them with?

A simple way to construct an I-statement is to use the following format as a guide.

"I feel _____ when you_____ because _____. I would really like it if _____ "

Practice using I statements. These can feel really awkward at first. Practicing them can make them feel easier and more natural over time.

Be clear. Say what you mean. People aren't mind readers and if they are left to assume what you mean, they will guess wrong about 50% of the time. Seriously, tell them what you think, feel, and need from them.

Talk in person. Texts or emails are easy to misinterpret. There's no context and all they have are the words. They can't hear your tone or see your body language. And, those matter.

Eye contact. Eye contact. Eye contact. Not looking someone in the eye can lead them to think you're trying to hide something.

Too much eye contact can feel weird and intimidating. So how much is enough? Basically, eye contact should feel comfortable for both people. It's ok to look away every few seconds and look back again.

Stay cool. Getting frustrated or angry is totally normal and it's part of resolving issues. What's not OK is saying ugly things and yelling. If you feel yourself getting upset and can't express your feelings calmly, take a break and cool off. Take a walk. Get some air. It's like a time-out. And it's awesome!

Apologize when you need to. No one is perfect and we all make mistakes. Saying you're sorry and meaning it can make an impossible situation all of a sudden fixable.

And, let me say one thing about apologizing. Apologizing isn't just for the other person. It is for you. If you've done something regrettable, the mature thing to do is apologize for your part. It lets the person know that you're worthy of forgiveness and compassion.

It doesn't make you appear weak. Oh no. It's a sign of immense strength because it takes courage to say, "Yes, I did that and I am sorry." You can't control what the other person does, but you can choose what you do. When you own your behavior, it's like making a deposit in your emotional bank.

So, now you have lots of communication tips. How do you use them?

A simple way to construct an I-statement is to use the following format as a guide.

"I feel _____ when you_____ because _____.
I would really like it if _____"

Practice here

Encouraging Healthy Conversations

Not everyone knows what you know now. A cool thing happens when one person uses healthy skills. A Lot of times, the other person will start to try as well. What that means is, if you are using good communication skills, it's likely the other person will try too. It might not be perfect but you have to start somewhere, right?

- Find a topic that you're both interested in. It can make talking easier when you can focus on something in common. Maybe you both like the same band or the same game. Start where you're comfortable.

- Show interest in the other person. Ask questions that allow them to share what they'd like to share. Be open to them asking you questions too.

- Be a good communication role model. Even if the other person isn't listening well, you do you. Use the skills you are learning to express yourself.

- Know when to step back. Sometimes things get heated. We talked about stepping back and taking a break. Sometimes the conversation just isn't going anywhere. That's ok too. It doesn't mean it was bad, maybe it was just meant to be short. It's ok to step back then too.

Remember, practice makes progress. Our interpersonal skills are always a work in progress but you now have a full set of communication skills you can try out.

—————————— **Now It's Your Turn** ——————————

Think about a conversation you had with someone recently that didn't go the way you wanted it to. Think about the communication skills you used and the ones you wish you'd used. Imagine having that conversation again.

- What might you say or do differently this time?

- What would you want this person to know?

- What skills would you try this time?

- Is it possible to have a talk with this person again? If so, consider going back with your new communication skills and try again.

Practice using your new communication skills. The next time you are interacting with someone, be mindful of your verbal and nonverbal communication. Notice the different ways people respond to you. Take time to reflect on what you did well and what seemed to not work so well. Remember, practice makes progress so keep working at it. As you become more comfortable with clear communication, the more successful you'll be.

If you're not sure where to start, start with the basics: calm facial expression, normal voice tone, good eye contact, listen to understand and remember your manners. Please, thank you, and kindness goes such a long way, especially when you're asking someone for something.

Let people see the awesome person you are!!

CHAPTER 4

Navigating Social Media

No discussion of teen life would be complete without talking about social media. Now, before you decide, "Oh, one more grown-up telling me why social media is so bad," hear me out. I think you might just be pleasantly surprised.

First, let me say that I think social media, and the internet in general, is one of the most influential and powerful things ever invented. It has opened doors and connected the world in ways generations before yours could barely imagine. Who would have thought that you could send a text to your mom and 5 minutes later do a video chat with someone halfway around the world that you met through online gaming? To say technology has come a long way would be an understatement.

Now, with that said, if we are going to keep it real, the internet and social media have their issues. There aren't safeguards built in and you have to be prepared to deal with a lot of sketchy stuff. The fact that you are interacting with people virtually means you only get a very tiny glimpse of who they might be or what they might be about. Notice that I said "might". You know and I know that when it comes to social media and the internet, what you "see" isn't always real and boundaries can get blurred. Guard up.

Social media is a powerful influence, especially for teens. There's an old saying, "With great power comes great responsibility." You probably recognize that quote from Spiderman. Actually, similar sentiments such as "with success comes responsibility" can be found all the way back to the Ancient Greeks. Basically, what that quote means is that wherever you find successful or powerful people or things, in this case, the internet and social media, there are responsibilities that come along with it.

For example, you're probably driving or about to be able to drive. When you get the keys and drive off, you have a responsibility to drive safely and not hurt yourself or someone else.

Same thing with social media. You have to use it with care so that you don't hurt someone or allow yourself to be harmed.

Yes, social media is fun. And it should be. It's also kind of like the wild west. You have to stay aware.

OK, that's my take on social media. It's a part of life to be managed. The goal is to use it safely and in ways that can help you live your best life. So, let's talk smart social media management.

Parents, Teens, and Social Media - It's Complicated

It's no secret teens and parents don't always see eye-to-eye on social media. It doesn't mean that either of you is all right or all wrong. You see it in different ways. You, as a teen, view things through the filter of a teen's experience. Totally normal. It's who you are. Your parents view things through the filter of an adult and parent. They have had different experiences. A lot of times, you might even agree about some things but still, approach them differently. That's ok. Normal and honestly, it's part of the parent-teen relationship that helps to guide you into adulthood.

Take a minute and think about the discussions you've had with your parents about social media. Do you agree on some things or is it a standoff? I'm encouraging you to think about this because as we go through this chapter, you may find things that you want to change about your social media use or discuss with your parents.

To say social media is a big part of teen life is an understatement. According to teen surveys, it's huge.

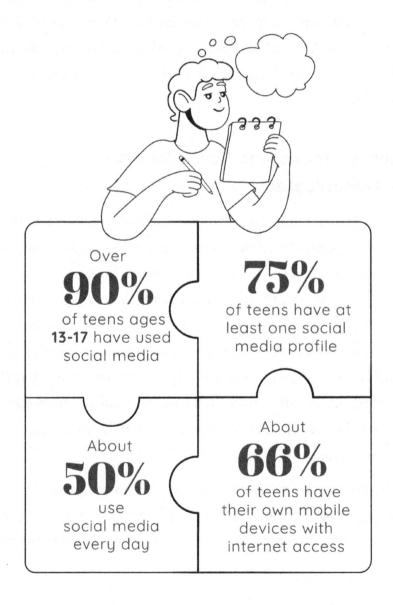

Over
90%
of teens ages
13-17 have used
social media

75%
of teens have at
least one social
media profile

About
50%
use
social media
every day

About
66%
of teens have
their own mobile
devices with
internet access

Teens love social media for so many reasons. Some really smart people have studied this love of social media and here's some of what teens told them:

- It's a technology you grew up with so it's comfortable and familiar

- It's cool to have instant access to people

- You like being able to share pictures or thoughts or important life moments

- It's a key part of how you connect with others and maintain relationships

- It's a place to be creative

- You tend to equate social media use with positive emotions

Have you ever thought about why you like social media?

Social media can feel like having a ginormous circle of friends. Someone is always available to connect with and you can share any part of your life you want. Of course, many of these friends are virtual friends but there's a sense of connection and inclusion that can be very appealing and comforting.

What's even more awesome is that smart people who study social media have found that social media use has lots of potential benefits that reflects a lot of what teens say about why the mad love for social media:

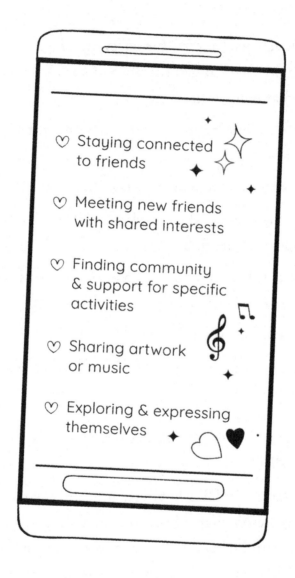

So how do parents see social media? Differently for sure but that's to be expected. Some other smart people asked parents what they think about their kids and social media use. Here's some of what parents are concerned about:

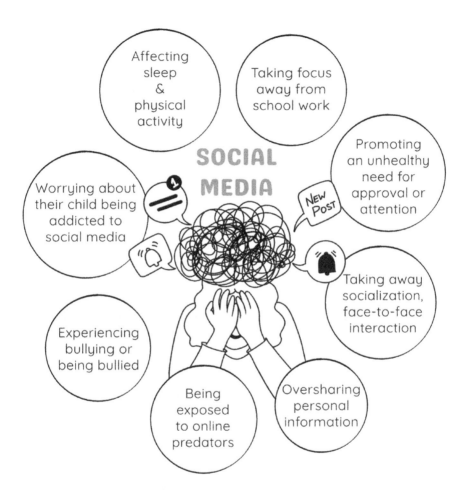

No surprises here, parents tend to worry about how social media might be affecting their teen's physical and emotional wellbeing. There is a lot of research that says these things can be real issues with social media so they're not looking for monsters under the bed. Does it happen to every kid? Of course not. But the risks are real. And, of course, parents worry about people who prey on kids. Don't be too hard on your parents on this one because the fact is, it does happen, even when you think you're being careful. Parents just worry about their kids so know that they aren't trying to get in your social media business just to be annoying. Their job is to help you get to adulthood healthy, happy, and safe.

Parents do acknowledge that there are good things about social media too. And, let's be totally upfront. Parents use social media too – a lot. And yes, they run into some of the same issues you might – spending too much time online, mean people, oversharing.

The fact is, there are true risks and benefits depending on how you handle your social media. For example, yes, you have a big circle to connect with but you don't know every single person beyond their profile pic and what they choose to share. And if there's one truth in social media it's that what you see isn't always what you're getting.

Social media is part of everyday life now and here to stay. The key to making it work for you and being part of your healthy life is to learn how to manage it. Let's look at some of the best ways to do that.

Manage Your Social Media Like a Boss

When you decide to take control of your social media, you open up the opportunity to get the best of what social media can offer. Remember I mentioned the benefits? You can't get the benefits of social media if you're engaged in risky, negative, or dangerous stuff. And, if social media is hurting you in some way, you know there's a good chance mom or dad will step in and manage it for you. Again, it's their job to protect you from those decisions that leave us wondering, "What were you thinking?"

Before we talk about the tips, let me say this: if you're living at home under your parents' care, your parents have a say in your social media use. It's not my "recommendation". It is just the reality of being a teen. You're not yet an adult so there are some things you can't control. The "it's private", "It's my phone", or other similar arguments go straight out the window. Sure, it's tempting to pull the "it's mine" argument but that usually puts you on the losing end. Trust me, NOT the deal you want to take.

When I was 16, I had a car that I worked every summer to get. Back in the day, a 16-year old couldn't own a car. I got a little fast and loose with my curfew and one night, an hour late, my dad calmly said, "You're grounded. Give me the keys" as I tried to sneak in the house. I tried the "It's mine" argument. He calmly reminded me he signed for it, registered it, and I was living in his home. The more I argued, the less willing he was to discuss it with me. And looking back, I don't blame him. I was a 16 year old spouting off about how I was mature and blah, blah, blah while basically throwing a temper tantrum like a 5 year old. Yeah, real mature and I wouldn't have given me the keys either. The takeaway? Parents do have authority and they step in when we do bonehead things. That's been teen life probably since cave-dwelling teens were drawing dinosaurs on rocks.

Now, I totally advocate for respect for privacy and not getting up in someone's business but the fact is, when it comes to their kids, parents will go to great lengths to protect them if they sense danger. Your parents have a job to protect you. If they think you're being secretive or sketchy, it sets off their parent radar. When that happens, you can bet you'll be handing over the phone or asked for your account passwords. They're not being mean. They're scared for you. I am including some tips for parents who have teens in a later chapter so that hopefully, these dramatic scenes don't happen.

So, with that said, my best social media management advice is:

1 *Have "the talk" with your parents about social media.* What do you think is reasonable? What are their expectations of you? If you start here and have the discussion, it's far less likely to come back and bite you later. Now, if you agree to a set of boundaries, it's important to follow through. That sends the message to your parents that they can trust you. And trust me. Trust is easier to keep than it is to earn back. (It took me what felt like a lifetime to get my keys back.)

2 *Practice transparency with your parents.* Sure, you want to have some privacy. And, most parents want to trust you. One of the ways you can really gain trust with your parents is to allow them access to your accounts. Give them your passwords. Expect that they might take a peek now and then. When they know they can check on you and they see that you're doing the right thing, conflicts are less likely to happen. Having some oversight is also helpful if you find yourself in a situation online. Remember, teens, don't do a great job of being able to see the nuances of a situation or see around corners. Your brain isn't there yet. Mom and dad have the benefit of being able to see what you might not. It's ok to let them help you.

3 *Be authentic.* Whether you're online or face-to-face with someone, it's important to be authentic in who you are. Yes, you can hide behind a keyboard but what that does to your confidence and self-esteem is damaging. And, keeping up a fake front is exhausting!

4 *Set limits for screen time.* There really is such a thing as too much screen time. And, it can interfere with your time management, your focus, even your sleep. How much is too much? That depends on how it affects you. A good place to start is to make sure your responsibilities are taken care of first – homework, chores, etc. This is a place where parents may have some rules in place like no phone at the dinner table or homework before social media time. This goes hand-in-hand with setting expectations with mom and dad.

5 *Be respectful to others.* Have you ever tried to talk to someone and they're staring at their phone? You KNOW they probably only heard about half of what you said. How did that feel to you? Remember the good communication skills we talked about? Looking at someone when they're speaking and giving them your full attention is part of active listening. And, it lets them know you respect them.

6 *Stay out of the drama.* There are going to be times when you will want to go off on someone. You might be tempted to drag someone who has wronged you. Resist that urge. Not only does it suck the energy out of you, but it also puts you smack in the middle of the drama. These social media battles escalate real quick and accomplish nothing. The keyboard bullies come crawling out and the backlash can be vicious. Nothing is worth your emotional health. As the saying goes, "Don't start a mess and there won't be any." Let. It. Go.

7 *Guard your privacy.* This one is a huge safety step. You don't always know who you're connecting with and information can be mined so easily. Protect as much as you can.

Use your privacy settings.
Be mindful of who you allow
to see your social media.

Never share addresses,
telephone numbers, social
security numbers, passwords,
financial information.

Turn your location
services off.

8 *Don't post or send anything you would be embarrassed for others to see.* Private has a whole different meaning when it comes to social media and the internet. Once you post or send something, even to someone you think is "safe", it is out there forever.

That sexy selfie you thought was so cool to send to your boyfriend or girlfriend is out there forever. Are you sure they won't repost it? You don't know who might see it or screenshot it or where or when it might resurface. Not worth the risk.

That mean rant you posted about someone who wronged you is now out there for the world to see. Do you really want someone to see that in 5 years when you're trying to land that dream job? It will still be there. Even if you deleted it, do you really want to gamble that the person you dragged on social media didn't screenshot it? "This is who you're hiring" is NOT the message you want posted to a potential employer's page. The news is full of these cases.

A very wise person once told me that before I wrote, printed, or posted anything, I should ask myself, "How comfortable would I be if this ends up on the news?" If you wouldn't want it to be all over the internet for all to see (even your family, future boss, or future spouse) then you probably don't want to post it.

9 *Build a positive identity online.* One of the cool things about the internet is that you can learn so much about someone. Colleges and employers have started using the internet and social media as ways of learning more about potential applicants. From the very first post you make, think about what you want people to know about you. Share your positive activities and experiences that show who you are. You never know who might be looking at your profile. Let them see your confidence, your strength, and your integrity. Focusing on the positives also boosts your self-esteem and self-worth.

10 *Don't hang out with the wrong crowd.* This is good advice whether you're online or not. Be careful with who you allow into your social circle. A few shady folks can put your privacy at risk and maybe even your reputation or your safety. Having 10K followers is not a measure of how well you're liked. It's like a friend collection of people you probably don't even know. Every now and then, go through your friend list and purge the ones you really don't know or don't really trust. You won't miss them.

11 ***Undershare.*** Be careful of falling into the oversharing trap. Social media can feel like a warm circle of friends, but the fact is, most everyone is all up in their own business and less interested in what you or anyone else is doing. But we think they are just wait-ing to like, share, or comment. When that doesn't happen, it can feel like a huge letdown. "Where're my likes???" It's an invitation for you to kick your self-esteem. A selfie or a post is fine but if you're posting your meals, your favorite memes, and every time you pee, ask yourself, "what am I needing?" Chances are, you might need some social time with friends or something to occupy extra time or a break. Waiting on likes won't fill that need.

So, there you have it. Everything you need to know about handling social media in a healthy, affirming way.

Social media can be fun and useful if managed well. It definitely requires respect and careful management to avoid falling into destructive relationships or patterns.

Have fun but protect yourself too.

I'm not the only grown-up who thinks managing your social media is a good idea. The American Academy of Pediatrics actually recommends that kids and parents make a social media plan. This allows you to have access to your social media and your parents to know that you are using it safely. You can see more about their recommendations on the Academy of Pediatrics website.

Below, I will give you some tips for making a plan with your parents. You want your social media. Your parents want to know you're using it safely. It all goes back to that communication and building trust with each other. It's a magical thing.

Now It's Your Turn

Think about your own social media experiences and patterns of use. What are the biggest challenges you face with your social media? What are the biggest issues or sticking points you have with your parents regarding social media?

Using the tips, what are some ways you could address those challenges? Make a social media plan. Share it with your parents so they know you are trying to use social media responsibly.

Here is a sample Social Media Plan. How yours looks might be a little different depending on you and your parents. The important thing here is for both of you to be clear about HOW you'll use social media responsibly. You want to use it in ways that are healthy and safe. Parents want to know you're ok. Having a social media plan isn't a punishment. It's more like a safeguard or safety net.

SAMPLE

Social Media Plan

This agreement is between me ___*Richard*___ and my parents ___*mom and dad*___ to be clear about the way I will use social media.

What I'm Using

I am currently using the following Apps and Services:

☒ Facebook   ☒ Instagram   ☐ TikTok

☐ Twitter   ☐ WhatsApp   ☐ Netflix

☒ YouTube   ☐ SnapChat   ☐ Kik

☐ _____   ☐ _____   ☐ _____

Expectations for Use

1. I will use social media only after my homework and other responsibilities are done.

2. I will put my phone away for the night at ___*10 pm*___. My phone will be on the charger in the ___*kitchen*___ (specify where you will leave your phone).

3. My parents may check my social media use for safety purposes. I agree to share my passwords with them when requested.

4. Parents agree to be respectful of my social media use. They will check it for safe use:

☐ Daily if there is a safety concern or suspected misuse

☒ Weekly

☐ Bi-weekly

☐ As needed

5. I agree to not create secret social media accounts.

6. I agree to not share personal information that could place me or my family in danger on social media.

7. I agree to use social media responsibly and avoid bullying or dangerous interactions of any kind.

8. Other expectations of parents or of teens (you can both add here)

You:_____   Date: _____

Parent:_____   Date: _____

Take time to review your contract and talk about how it's working. You can revise it together as you need to. The idea of the contract is to have a safe monitoring practice in place that allows you the freedom to use social media while allowing your parents to monitor for safety.

CHAPTER 5

Managing Social Anxiety

As a teen, whenever I was around other people, I always wondered, "What do they think of me? Do they think I'm weird?" I felt weird, that's for sure. For as long as I can remember, I always felt like "that kid". You know, the one. The one that never spoke up or raised his hand in class. The one that always looked lost and never seemed to get noticed. The one that didn't draw attention to himself or go out for sports. The one who wanted to go to HOCO and prom so badly but was scared to death to ask anyone. What if they said no?

I wanted so badly to fit in, to feel like I was like everyone else. I wanted to be outgoing like my peers and do all the fun things

I saw them doing. But, for me, social situations were so hard. I struggled with what to say or do. But no matter how I tried, I always just felt awkward. It became easier to just keep my distance and hope someone would see me.

I didn't really understand all the why's. I just knew I was unhappy and feeling alone. I'd get so nervous! I felt like I was the only one. Looking back, I now know that what I was experiencing was social anxiety. And, I wish I'd known then what I know now.

Does this sound like you? If so, you're not alone. Anxiety in teens is really common. In fact, about 1 in 3, or about 33%, of teens struggle with anxiety. Social anxiety, one of the most common kinds of anxiety, accounts for about 10% of teen anxiety, maybe more. In any case, that's a lot of teens with anxiety. You probably have friends who deal with anxiety too.

Recognizing anxiety can be confusing too. Using the term *"anxiety"* as in "I have anxiety right now" or *"panic"* as in "dude, I'm having a panic attack", has just become part of everyday language. What people are usually trying to say is that they're feeling nervous or anxious about something. Experiencing some normal anxiety – we all get nervous, sometimes really nervous, about something which is actually normal and usually, it passes. But, for some people, that nervousness becomes a problem.

Living with anxiety can be hard. It can hold you back from doing things you want to do. It can embarrass you. And, anxiety likes to lie to you. Anxiety makes you feel like there's something wrong with you and that you're the only one who feels the way you do. Both of those assumptions are lies. You are not alone. And, more importantly, there's nothing wrong with you.

Read that again:

THERE IS NOTHING WRONG WITH YOU.

In this chapter, we're going to take a deeper dive into anxiety. It's more than "having a panic attack" or being nervous before you have to present your project in class or ask that special someone to HOCO.

And, we will talk about what anxiety looks like in teens like you. Your anxiety is not like a grown-up's anxiety and it can look different.

We will talk about things you can DO about your anxiety. It's one thing to talk about it but if you don't do something about it, the anxiety goes on and continues to bug you.

Anxiety doesn't go away completely, and we wouldn't want it to. Some anxiety is good and keeps you moving forward in life. It stems from the most primitive parts of the brain, sometimes referred to as the reptile brain. This part of your brain is part of your "early warning system" that activates when it senses danger. It helps us run away when we need to. It keeps us from doing dangerous things. It saved our ancestors from being eaten by dinosaurs.

Anxiety becomes a problem when it sticks around. For some reason, it doesn't turn off. It starts to interfere with your life and mess with your head. Dealing with anxiety is about turning down that response because not every day is a day to run from dinosaurs.

Wouldn't it be nice to be able to feel confident and hopeful and excited to start each day? To try new things? And to not worry about fitting in or saying something wrong or feeling isolated? *To. Just. Relax.* It can happen. There are things you can do to make it happen.

Let's jump in!

What is Social Anxiety?

Social anxiety is a kind of anxiety that happens in response to social situations. It can happen before, during, or even after the situation or all three. Some social anxiety is *completely* normal and almost all of us are shy or nervous around others sometimes. Meeting new people, having to give a speech or presentation (ugh, for me it was standing up in class to give my presentation), a college interview, asking someone out on a date are just a few of the biggest anxiety-producing situations. Then, we worry about what people thought of us, did we do it right? And, most of us feel relieved. Whew! That's over!

There's another side of social anxiety that isn't as noticeable. It shows up in a million little ways. Here are just a few common examples:

SIGNS OF SOCIAL ANXIETY

* Not wanting to answer the phone

* Not raising your hand in class

* Walking the long way around to avoid a crowd of people

* Not attending dances, sports events, and other school activities

* Avoiding the use of public bathrooms

* Struggling to start a conversation or engage in one

* Not asking someone out on a date

* Avoiding eye contact

* Avoiding talking to someone you don't know

Do you see yourself in any of these examples? What situations do you avoid? What other actions can you think of that you use to avoid social contact or uncomfortable situations?

A lot of these examples are things we might all do now and then. And, they are not dramatic examples. So, a lot of times, someone's social anxiety may be overlooked as just the shyness or awkwardness of being a teen.

Think about it: adolescence is the time in your life when you're expanding your social circle, you're maturing and beginning to date and taking on new responsibilities. All these things require you to interact more often and with more people. You're learning new ways of interacting and you're going to be awkward sometimes.

Sometimes, people start avoiding social situations out of fear of being judged or embarrassed. It's when the anxiety keeps you from doing things you want to do or affects your social functioning that it becomes a problem.

And, if you're looking for ways to be more socially comfortable and engaged, yeah, your anxiety is bugging you.

For some people, that worry and nervousness just won't turn off. The worry can become so intense that their brain decides, "Nope, just going to avoid that." The anxiety starts a cycle of avoiding lots of other things too.

What Keeps Social Anxiety Happening?

To understand why social anxiety keeps happening to you, you have to understand how it starts in the first place. When you understand something, it's less scary and you can figure out what to do about it.

Social anxiety, like other forms of anxiety, has its roots in our primitive "fight or flight" response. When your brain detects a "social threat" of some kind, it sets off alarms that something catastrophic is going to happen. It might be the risk of being embarrassed. It might be the fear of being rejected by that desired HOCO date. How intense that anxiety response will be depends on a couple of things: how likely it is that what we fear will happen and how bad we think it would be if our fears came true. All this happens in your brain in milliseconds.

If you worry that you'll be too nervous to get the words out and laughed at by your HOCO date, then the alarm is sounded. Danger! Danger!

The neurochemicals are flowing and you probably feel your anxiety rising. Many people experience these sensations as shakiness, sweating, heart racing, and an intense need to escape. Your brain is screaming "Get the heck outta there!"

It's the same response you'd use if you were being chased by a dinosaur. Thanks, biology!

But you're not being chased by a dinosaur and you can't always run away. So, what do you do instead? You recognize all these sensations as anxiety. You get sucked into those negative thought loops we talked about earlier and you start to avoid what you fear. Over time, your anxiety gets triggered over and over by similar fears. You start to develop what's known as avoidance behaviors to try and avoid those fears.

Now, sometimes, avoidance can be helpful. Say on the day you wanted to ask your friend to HOCO, you were just not feeling well or you'd had a really bad day and you were just crazy nervous. You had a feeling it wouldn't end well. You decided to try again tomorrow. Perfectly acceptable and probably a smart move.

But what happens when avoidance behaviors become the way you deal with anxiety? It becomes your go-to response because you never get past it to face those fears in healthy ways. Or, find out those fears were completely unfounded and not real at all. The social fears are still there. It becomes a destructive cycle of trigger, anxiety response, avoidance. On repeat. Over time, that avoidance creates more and more social anxiety because you start to believe that you just can't cope socially. Hello, social anxiety.

What are your anxiety triggers? What social situations create anxiety for you? Are there some that are worse than others? Are there some situations that you try to avoid completely? What are the fears you have about them?

Negative Thinking

As with other areas of life, negative thinking plays a huge role in how we cope with things. Social anxiety is no different.

Negative thoughts about social situations are one of the reasons people feel socially anxious. Some of these negative thoughts are experienced as words (kind of like that inner dialogue). Others are experienced as images or visual memories. You may remember what someone said or did. You might focus on the what-ifs of future social situations. Whatever the form, these negative thoughts can feed your social anxiety, keeping you fearful and isolated.

Core Beliefs

Core beliefs are strongly held beliefs about ourselves and others and the world. They are rooted in some of our earliest experiences and shape the way we perceive what happens to us. Many people with social anxiety disorder recall early life events that were associated with significant social anxiety.

For example, say you were in the class play when you were in Kindergarten. Maybe you had to get up on stage and recite some lines. (I think most of us have had to do something like that.) It's a scary moment for a little one. Now, say you got up there and forgot the words. You may not remember the exact moment, but you might remember your teacher's face, your friends snickering, or even your own sense of "I messed up."

Sometimes, those experiences roll off like water off a duck's back. Sometimes, though, they stick with us. For whatever reason, they become part of our sense of self and part of how we perceive the world. And, remember that confirmation bias from chapter one? Yeah, over time, we start to believe we can't do something or we're not "good" or "smart" or what-  ever, and our minds go looking for that "proof" in the world around us. It's a vicious cycle that can send your anxiety off the charts. It starts to whisper, "No, don't do it. They'll laugh.", "No one is interested in what I have to say." "I'll mess it up."

I've been there and I get it. And, there are things you can do to get that anxiety in check.

So what do we do about these negative ways of thinking? More importantly, how can you stop your social anxiety from jamming up your style?

Take Control of Your Social Anxiety

It may not feel like it and your anxiety may tell you otherwise, but you CAN take control of your social anxiety. It takes some time and some practice but you can shift the way you think. And when you shift the way you think, you start to shift the way you act. So, let's take a closer look. Just FYI, you might want to take notes.

Changing Negative Thinking Patterns

First, check that inner self-talk. Remember that inner voice we talked about in chapter one? Yeah, that one. It's time to reset that loop. Your thoughts drive so much of what you do.

The thoughts that go through your head, that ongoing dialogue, when you're face-to-face with one of your triggers, become so ingrained that they become your go-to response. They trigger those feelings of anxiety and insecurity and all those uncomfortable feelings. In turn, you choose actions to try and avoid or alleviate that distress. And then here come the thoughts again.

Here's an example:

Say having to speak in class is super anxiety-provoking for you. Think about times when you've had to speak in front of your class.

So, it makes sense to change those negative thought patterns that keep you stuck.

> **Thoughts:** *What kinds of thoughts usually go through your mind in a situation like that? What is that inner voice saying to you?*
>
> **Feelings:** *What feelings usually come up for you in situations like that? Are there physical sensations that happen? (For example, sweaty palms, racing heart, shaky hands, etc.)*
>
> **Actions:** *When you find yourself in this position and are feeling anxious, what do you usually do?*

OK, so what can you do about these negative thoughts? You challenge them. As you challenge those negative thoughts, you are training your brain to learn to cope with those trigger situations.

Now, you might be tempted to just ignore them and hope they go away, or worse, just keep giving in to them. Have you ever tried to ignore something someone has told you not to? It's like when you were little and your parents told you don't touch the vase on the coffee table. Guess what? Chances are, you tried to touch it every chance you got until they moved it.

The key to changing your thoughts is to challenge them, face them head-on. As you learn to challenge your negative thoughts, your challenge gives way to more positive thoughts and a healthier way to cope. Challenge essentially shuts the negativity down. When you take the power away from the trigger, anxiety has nowhere to go.

Here's an example using the class presentation example:

You: I'm going to get up there and not know what to say.

Challenge your thinking: How do I know that's going to happen?

Coping thinking: I've prepared for my presentation. I have some things I can say even if I don't remember all of them.

Think about some other situations that trigger your social anxiety. Try the challenge and see what you come up with. It might feel kind of weird at first because you're asking your brain to do something different. When you find yourself in a situation, try the challenge. Remember, practice makes progress.

Here's a reminder:

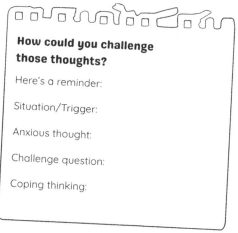

How could you challenge those thoughts?

Here's a reminder:

Situation/Trigger:

Anxious thought:

Challenge question:

Coping thinking:

Practice Breathing Exercises

This one may sound kind of odd for a social anxiety tip but breathing, besides just keeping us alive, influences so much of our body and mind.

You might not notice it, but when you get anxious, you tend to breathe more rapidly. You might also feel more tense, your heart rate might increase, you might start to sweat, or feel like something bad is going to happen. Even your thoughts might start to race. What the heck is going on?? It's that fight-or-flight response again.

Remember, your brain is hard-wired to react to what it perceives as distress or danger. Your breathing increases to move oxygen more quickly to your muscles and your heart is pumping faster too so that your muscles are ready to go if you need to. Your brain treats danger the same whether it's a T-Rex or having to introduce yourself to someone.

One thing we know from those smart science people is that deep breathing brings that response down and induces a state of calmness. Breathing techniques also help to reduce worry, and calm and quiet the mind. Basically, breathing helps your body and your brain to relax.

Now, you might be thinking, "I already know how to breathe." Well, of course, you do. What we're talking about here is using your breath as a TOOL to help you relax and, in those times when your anxiety is running hot, to bring it down so you can get through those moments.

I'm going to share a technique that really helped me. It's a technique called 4-7-8, also known as "relaxing breath". It's called 4-7-8 because of the pattern of breathing it uses. Essentially, you breathe in for 4 seconds, hold your breath for 7 seconds, and release your breath by exhaling for 8 seconds. This technique can be used to reduce anxiety or to help relax before sleep.

Here's how you do it:

4-7-8 BREATHING

Step 1.
Find a place to sit quietly.
Place the tip of your tongue on the
back of your upper teeth.
Keep it there while you're breathing.
This takes some practice.

Step 2.
With your lips parted,
exhale completely through your
mouth, making a whooshing sound.

Step 3.
Now, close your mouth and inhale
slowly through your nose
as you count to 4 in your head.

1-2-3-4

1-2-3-4-5-6-7

Step 4.
Hold your breath as you
count to 7 in your head.

Step 5.
Exhale through your mouth making
a whooshing sound for 8 seconds.

8 secs

Box Breathing

Box breathing is a deep breathing technique used for relaxation and anxiety reduction. It's so effective it's even used by the United States Navy Seals!

Also called "square breathing", it's called box breathing in reference to the fact that a box has four sides and is represented by this technique's pattern of 4 count breathing for a total of four times.

Here's how to box breathe:

BOX BREATHING

1. Find a comfortable place to sit.
Take your time and breathe at your own pace.
There is no right or wrong pace.

2. Gently exhale, letting out all of the air in your lungs for a count of 4.

3. Keep your lungs empty for a count of 4.

4. Gently inhale for a count of 4.

5. Keep your lungs full for a count of four.

6. Exhale and repeat 2 or 3 times.

Just a tip: It can be hard to know how fast or slow to breathe. One trick that lots of people use is a count of "One Mississippi", "Two Mississippi", and so on.

Take A Chance on YOU

So, we've talked about challenging the negative thinking that feeds anxiety and we've talked about how to bring those anxious feelings down. That's all fine and good but now you have to DO something.

A huge part of overcoming social anxiety is learning to do something different. Feeding into your anxiety keeps you from doing the things you want to do by avoiding them, right? Overcoming social anxiety includes learning how to do the things you want to do. And it might not feel like it, but YOU CAN DO IT!

Now, I am not Pro "jump in the deep end". Nope. I found the best way to learn how to overcome my social anxiety and live the life I wanted was to take small steps towards what I wanted. I had to do something different.

Here's my story:

I saw my friends going places and doing the things I only dreamed of. I wanted to go to games and dances and hang out with my friends. I didn't want to feel left out. I didn't want to be afraid to talk to someone I liked. I was learning new skills but now what? I had to start using them. But how?

Ladders. Think of your social anxiety as keeping you from something you want. It's just out of reach. A ladder can help you reach. A really awesome therapist introduced me to something called Exposure Ladders. It's kind of a technical way of saying, "take small steps towards what you want to do." An exposure ladder, sometimes called a fear ladder, is a list of the things or situations you fear, listed from the least scary to the most scary. Without getting all technical, the idea is to take something you're fearful of, in this case, something that provokes your social anxiety, and break it down into small steps that over time, move you closer to what you want. The idea is to move a bit out of your safe zone, take a step, take the next step...slowly until you reach the top rung of the ladder.

It's kind of a fancy social anxiety "to-do" list.

So how does this idea work?

Here's an example:

Say you want to invite someone to HOCO. The idea of asking that someone out makes you so nervous you just can't. But you really want to go with this person. So, the goal (top rung of your ladder) is to ask the person to HOCO. Think about some smaller steps that are less anxiety-provoking that might get you there. Your ladder might look something like this:

TOP - Ask the person to HOCO 10

Ask the person to study for the math test together 8

Text the person 7

Sit next to the person in class or at lunch and start a conversation about something familiar like math class or something happening at school 5

Say Hi when you pass each other. Don't forget to make eye contact when you say hi. 4

The numbers you see are a rating of how uncomfortable each step might be. Lowest to highest.

Of course, your steps or ratings might be different. This is just an example. You can use this step-by-step with lots of situations. The idea is to *DO SOMETHING* that moves you closer to your goal in a way that won't make you jump out of your skin or say, "Oh heck no. I'm out."

What's a situation that you've been avoiding and wanting to overcome but just can't find the place to start? What might your ladder look like for this situation?

Now It's Your Turn

Pick a situation that you've been avoiding and want to try and overcome.

Identify what triggers your anxiety about the situation?

What are the negative thoughts that stop you from doing what you want to do?

How could you challenge those thoughts?

Here's a reminder:

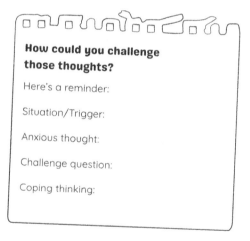

How could you challenge those thoughts?

Here's a reminder:

Situation/Trigger:

Anxious thought:

Challenge question:

Coping thinking:

Now, try making a ladder to reach your goal. At the end of the book, you'll find a section with a Steps to Success form. You can use that template as your guide. You'll see spaces for your steps. You'll see oval spaces to add your difficulty ratings. You might have 3 steps. You might have more than 5 or 6. It is totally up to you and what steps you feel comfortable taking. Remember: It's ok if it's not perfect and it's ok to ask for help from a friend or trusted adult. When you're ready, try your first step.

CHAPTER 6

We Have A Situation

"What do I do about..." is a phrase that people young and old find themselves saying all the time. It's one thing to learn lots of tips and tricks and even understand yourself a little better. It's a whole other thing to figure out how to use that info. I was the same as you. I learned everything I could about my own way of being and the changes I wanted to see. But then, I had to figure it all out. Now what?

This chapter is the one I wish someone had written for me. It would have saved me an awful lot of time bouncing around trying to navigate the bumps in my life. So, I decided to dedicate a chapter to some of the more common struggles or situations teens like you might find yourself in and offer you some tips for dealing with them.

Now, let me say, everyone is different. Your situation might not be exactly like someone else's. That's ok. Chances are, you've encountered something similar and find yourself saying, "I wish I'd known then what I know now" or "Hey, why didn't anyone tell me about that?" That's what this chapter is about.

I decided to take some real deal situations that, as a teen, you're likely to encounter. I break them down and highlight the decision points all along the way. It's these decision points where you can decide to do something to move yourself to a more positive, healthy place or stay stuck. Sometimes, it isn't always easy to see where the decision points are, or what the right decision for you is.

Situation 1: Feeling Comfortable Around Peers or in Social Situations

This situation is a common one. There are going to be times when you feel just out of place or uncomfortable. It happens to everyone. But, knowing that doesn't make it any easier does it. Nor does someone just telling you to suck it up and deal with it. Honestly, that used to just make it harder for me. If I knew how to "just suck it up", I would have already done it, right?

If you already struggle with some self-esteem or anxiety issues, feeling comfortable around peers or other social settings can be challenging. I want to offer you some tips to help get through those situations. Some of the tips might work for you. Others might not, and that's ok. Use what works for you. Remember that personality stuff we talked about? Not everyone is the same and what works for one person just might not be what is right for another person.

So, here are some strategies you can try:

Know your triggers. Knowing what kinds of situations are really hard for you is important. You might not be able to always avoid them, and you probably won't want to. Often we avoid it because we don't know what else to do.

When you know what triggers makes you feel uncomfortable, you can either work around them or have a plan to manage them. For example, group activities might make you self-conscious or uncomfortable. You know you have a group project that will be a big part of your grade. Blowing it off is a bad idea, right? So, instead, maybe you volunteer for the parts of the project that don't feel so uncomfortable.

Make it a point to say hi to your group partners when you see them. We tend to be more comfortable around people we are familiar with.

Practice visualizing participation in the group. We will talk more about visualization in Chapter 7. Visualizing success is something athletes do all the time. When you see yourself doing something in your head, when it comes time to actually do it, your brain says, "Oh we know how. We got this!" Now, this is a really simple explanation but the point is, mental rehearsing helps us to be less anxious. Remember, anxiety is about worrying about what hasn't happened yet. When you use mental rehearsal, your brain is already prepared.

Use your breathing exercises. When you start feeling anxious, take a few slow, deep breaths. Feel your body relax and your mind settle.

If you feel comfortable, ask one of the group members to help you if you get stuck. After all, you're all in it together. At least one of them is probably feeling anxious too.

Situation 2: Speaking So You Feel Heard

Expressing yourself can be really hard and sometimes, the right words just won't come. In your head, thoughts are spinning and you can't get them into words. Your anxiety is off into the "what ifs".

First, stop what you're doing and take some breaths. Try some box breathing or the 4-7-8 technique. Let your body and mind relax.

Next, take a few minutes to think about what you need to say. What are the main points you want to get across? Write it down if you need to.

> **FUN FACT:** Did you know writing things down helps us to focus on and remember them better? Yup. It's all in the way your brain stores information.

When you speak, stand up tall, make good eye contact with the person, and use your "I-statements." "I think...", "I need...". Check your body language. You want it to be open so that the other person sees you as approachable. Check your voice tone. Are you speaking in a calm, neutral tone or are you yelling, demanding, or being sarcastic? Let's be honest here - if you're talking with your fists balled up or your arms flailing all over and hurling F-bombs, chances are people are backing away. And, they've already stopped listening.

The other side of this is not speaking loud enough. Sometimes when you feel insecure or unsure, your voice might get too soft. Then, the other person may not even hear you but you'll walk away feeling unheard. Use an assertive voice and look for signs that the person hears you. Are they looking at you? Nodding or responding? If not, try again.

Maintain your composure. If you start feeling nervous and struggle with what you want to say, take some deep breaths and try again. You might even need to take a break. It sounds funny but a "big kid time out" is da bomb! It is your BFF when you're struggling to express yourself. It's not a punishment or a sign of failure. Instead, it's a way for you to quietly regroup and try again BEFORE your anxiety psychs you out and you shut down.

Remember, practice makes progress. Try to use these skills whenever you're having a conversation with someone. Practice looking at people and using an assertive voice when you speak.

> **ANOTHER FUN COMMUNICATION FACT:** Making eye contact can be one of the HARDEST things to do. It takes up a lot of brainpower and it can kick off your anxiety. Making good eye contact takes practice. One cool tip from public speaking pros is to look just above someone's eyes. Sometimes looking directly into the eyes can be uncomfortable. As you practice, you'll get more comfortable.

Situation 3: Your First Job

Getting your first job is something that usually happens in your teens. While it's pretty exciting, it can also be a nerve wracker! First, you have to get through the interview. Then, if you get the job, you have to show up. So, here are some tips for getting through this teen rite of passage.

Prepare for your interview:

Accept that you're going to be nervous. That's normal. Be careful not to let your anxiety talk you out of going to the interview. It's just your fear of talking and you CAN do it!

Decide what is appropriate to wear. There's an old saying by the very wise Will Rogers, "You never get a second chance to make a first impression." You want your prospective employer to see you and think, "I want you working for me." Now, chances are a coat and tie, what my grandma used to call our "Sunday best", are probably more than you need for an interview. You do want to dress well though. Pajama pants are a hard NO. Same for fuzzy socks. Take a shower. Put on clean clothes.

Rehearse your interview. Think about and imagine how you'll meet your interviewer. Will you shake hands? (Maybe not because some social courtesies have changed with the pandemic.) Imagine how you will interact. Think eye contact, pleasant facial expressions (it's ok to smile), even posture. Slouching down in the chair is a no-go.

Be prepared for questions, too. Ask a friend or trusted adult to practice answering interview questions with you.

Don't forget to bring any documents you might need, like your ID or social security number, that you'll need for tax documents if you get the job.

Use your breathing exercises if you get nervous. Let the interviewer see how awesome you are! Now go get that job!

Handling the First Few Days on the Job:

You did it! You got the job and now you have to go. That can be the second hardest part. Now you're going to be meeting new people and learning new things. Your anxiety will probably be high and whispering, "Don't go. You can't do this." Oh yes, you can.

First jobs are a time for learning. Expect that you're going to make mistakes. It's normal. I made a ton of mistakes with my first job. And, looking back, I probably wasn't very good at it in the beginning. That's ok. None of us are with anything new. We learn by trial and error - by doing. The challenge is to let yourself learn from those mistakes.

So, here are some tips:

Get a good night's sleep. Good, restful sleep will help you feel refreshed and ready for the day. Sleep is also a great anxiety fighter.

Get up on time. This is one step that trips lots of us up, especially if you aren't used to getting up at that time. Leave yourself time to get dressed and prepare for the day.

Mentally rehearse if you're feeling anxious. Think about what you'll be doing on your first day.

When you arrive, say hi to the people you'll be working with if you haven't had a chance to already. Remember, we are more comfortable around people we're familiar with. If you're invited to sit with someone at your break, say yes.

Give yourself permission to become part of the work team. If you find your inner voice being negative, try using those challenging questions. For example, your inner voice might say, "They're not going to want me to sit by them." Challenge that! What evidence do you have that they would do that? Isn't it just as likely that they will ask you to join them? And follow up: I said hi to everyone so they know I am friendly. Even if they don't invite you, you know that you've opened the door. They may be feeling anxious too. Look for opportunities to be part of the group.

Chances are, you will have someone showing you the ropes the first few days. Ask questions. Use those active listening skills. Pay attention. It's easy to let yourself get overwhelmed and distracted.

If you find yourself feeling nervous, take some slow deep breaths and focus on what you're doing. When you focus on the present, you can't focus on the "what ifs" of what hasn't happened yet.

Situation 4: Dealing With All the Feels

Truth here: Being a teen is a rollercoaster time. You're learning about yourself and you're shaping your ideas about the world you live in. Add in the tremendous physical and emotional growth you're experiencing, and you'll probably find your feelings all over the place. That is TOTALLY NORMAL!

Those feelings can be pretty intense and even confusing. Sometimes, you might feel embarrassed that you're feeling so emotional. Being emotional is not a weakness and nothing to be embarrassed about.

Learn to identify your feelings. This sounds silly but many of us aren't really taught how to recognize, much less deal with feelings.

Think about this: if you ask someone how they feel, often you'll get "Good". You probably do it too. We all do. The problem with "good" is that good isn't a feeling. What does it really mean? And then, there's the vague, slightly cryptic, "I'm good." Are you?

A better way to deal with feelings is to get in the habit of naming your feelings. Take a minute a few times a day to check in: How am I feeling today?

If you're having a hard time, ask, "How am I feeling right now?" And then call it what it is. When you know what you're feeling, you're more likely to choose a helpful way to deal with it.

Being able to define what you're feeling also makes it easier to tell someone else how you're feeling. If you don't, they have to guess and I promise you, they will guess wrong AT LEAST half the time. We're humans. We are not mind readers. If you're asking someone for something, you want them to know how you feel so that they can understand what you're telling them. "I'm good" when you've got your feelings hurt doesn't let the other person know that you need some comfort or support - or maybe an apology. They can't read your mind.

If identifying feelings is hard for you, I have included a tool at the end of the book called the Feeling Wheel that was designed to help people identify feelings. It's not a complete list for sure but it's a tool that you can use to try and define your feelings.

Situation 5: Going Off to College or Moving to a New Town

Going out on your own is another of those teenage rites of passage. Sooner or later, almost all of us venture out into the world. Doing so for the first time can be scary, to say the least. It's also a grand adventure and the first step into your next phase of life - adulthood.

College or a first apartment is often the first venture out into the world. Sometimes that means moving to a new town. The  first thing to remember is, you are going to be nervous. That's ok. You're supposed to be. It's that good nervousness that keeps you moving in the right direction. Now, with that said, sometimes your anxiety can be pretty high with this kind of step. And, what happens when you get to where you're going can be anxiety-provoking too.

So, here are some tips for handling this big step:

Check out your new surroundings ahead of time. Visit a few times if you can. Getting familiar with a new place can make it seem not-so-unfamiliar when you make the move. Learn your way around. Know where the essential things are like grocery stores, gas stations, clinics, and the like. Google maps are awesome for this!

Google the fun spots! What's there to do in your new place? Find some things to do that you enjoy.

If you know someone where you're moving to, connect with them. Make some plans to get together. Ask about fun things to do. A familiar face is always a mind easer.

If you're new in town and don't know anyone, look for a group to join. It might be a running group or an organization on campus. Your school might offer different activities like movie nights or concerts or other fun things. Give yourself permission to go and check it out. Chances are, you're going to find some like-minded people to share the fun with. Say hi to people you meet whether it's at the grocery store or in your 3-hour chemistry lab. You never know where your next friendship will be made.

If you're not in school, there are still ways to connect in your new town. Look for community events that are of interest to you. And then go. Look for opportunities to volunteer for your favorite cause. Join a gym or a theater group. You will likely meet others who are new in town too. Say hi to people you meet along the way. Ask people for recommendations for fun and interesting things to do.

In any of these scenarios, remember to use your good communication and anxiety management skills. Breathe. Give yourself permission to be out there. Take those baby steps if you need to. The important thing is to resist the urge to avoid. This is an exciting time of your life and doors will open in places you never imagined. You want to be ready when they do.

Situation 6: Knowing When And How To Ask For Help

Spoiler alert: Asking for help is always a good choice.

We've talked a lot about managing anxiety and feelings. Breathing, taking small steps, rehearsing, and more. These are all great tips and a lot of times, with a little practice, you can overcome your insecurities and thrive.

Sometimes, though, despite your best efforts, you're still feeling stuck. Or, you're experiencing troubling thoughts or feelings. If you find yourself here, it's time to ask for help. And, there is no shame in it.

I know. Asking for help can be hard. I've been where you are. No one likes to admit they're struggling.

You want to be able to do it on your own. It can feel like a weakness to have to ask for help. Well, let me be blunt here:

Asking for help is NOT a sign of weakness. It is a sign of strength. When you allow yourself to ask for help, you are doing one of the most courageous and kind things that you can do for yourself. You are facing your fears and doing what you know to be right for you.

Sometimes, those around you who love and care for you will see you struggling before you realize you're in deep. They may step up and offer help. This is the other side of asking for help. Accepting help when it is offered is just as important and a just as powerful show of strength.

Finding Help

Finding help will depend on what you need. Most often, that will be a therapist. Now, let me say this as bluntly as I can. Seeing a therapist DOES NOT mean that you're "crazy" or "psycho" or any of those terms that people use. In fact, most people who see therapists are perfectly sane, regular people who are just struggling with some aspect of life. It can be hard to see our own behavior much less know what to do about it. And people close to us are sometimes too close. Or, it's too uncomfortable to share your personal feelings with them. Therapists can help you sort out all the feelings and thoughts and help you find ways to cope with whatever is troubling for you.

Therapy isn't like the old stereotype of going into an office, lying on the sofa, and talking for hours about your childhood. Nope. Therapy today is about helping you deal with what needs dealing with and finding ways to live your life healthy, happy, and the way you want it. With the rise of internet ther-apy, you don't even have to go sit in an office. You can do something called telehealth and see your therapist in a private, secure video session when it's convenient for you. And online therapy is proven to be as effective as in-the-office therapy.

All I can say is, I wish they would have had that option when I was a teen.

And one more thing I want to say about seeking help. It DOES NOT automatically mean you need to be on medicine. In fact, most people don't. There are some people who do need it and that's great. Despite what you might hear or see in the media, treating issues like anxiety or depression is NOT as simple as popping a pill. It's a decision to make in consultation with your doctor and your parents.

If you're feeling down and need someone to talk to, there is the National Suicide Prevention Lifeline. You can call or text 24/7 and talk to a trained counselor.

Voice 1-800-273-8255

Text HOME to 741741 from anywhere
in the United States, anytime.

CHAPTER 7

Manage Your Stress Before It Manages You

At first glance, you might think that a chapter on managing stress is just boring. (I can imagine your eyes rolling already.) You might even be tempted to skip over it. Before you do that, though, hear me out. There's a reason I included this chapter and even if you think it doesn't apply to you, chances are, by the time I finish explaining the why you will.

What's the Deal with Stress?

Stress is one of those things that you know when you feel it but it isn't always easy to put into words. You're probably familiar with terms like "stressed out" and that's how most people might think of stress.

When we talk about stress in the context of mental health and wellbeing, we're talking about stress as:

"a state of mental tension and worry caused by problems in your life, work, etc." or,

"something that causes strong feelings of worry or anxiety."

Remember when I said in the beginning that your generation is different than any generation before yours? Well, with each generation comes new advances in science, new technologies, and new ways of interacting with the world around you. Just 20 years ago, there was no social media. Cell phones were around but nothing like today's smartphones. Streaming services were not a thing yet and real-time chatting like Skype or Facetime? Nope.

Yours is the first generation to be *completely* linked into the world 24/7 and in REAL-TIME.

You can be sitting at your desk in Anywhere, USA, and chat face-to-face with someone in Anytown, Australia or Ukraine or England, or virtually anywhere else in the world.

You can watch world events as they unfold. You don't even have to wait to see it on the news. Chances are, someone is streaming live.

You can attend school virtually and even get a college degree without ever stepping into a classroom.

You have access to information and resources and people, places, and things unlike ever before.

24/7 news coverage and entertainment and live streaming take you virtually any place you want to go.

And, thanks to social media, you can connect with friends and share your world with whoever you choose.

All this sounds great, right? And it is. But with all of the new ways of living, brings a lot of pressure and expectations.

Unlike any generation before yours, you face tremendous pressure and expectations to "do" and "be" in certain ways. There's pressure to do well in school, to choose the "right" career, to have the "right" social media presence, to be the "best" (whatever that means), and to have whatever is most coveted by the "influencers" on social media...the list goes on and on.

I hear you...you're thinking, "He says this like this is a bad thing."

I'm not saying that any of this is a "good" thing or a "bad" thing. It simply is what is.

Think about this:

When you post something on social media, why do you do it? You want someone to see what you're doing. We all do. Then, how about those "likes" and "shares"? For a lot of teens, those acknowledgements mean something to them; they validate something for them. *Pressure. Expectations.*

When you're studying for your ACT or SAT, you feel the pressure to do well. Maybe your family has expectations for where you'll go to college or what you'll study. *Pressure. Expectations.*

When you're deciding what shoes to get for back to school. What's everyone wearing this year? Will I be cool enough? *Pressure. Expectations.*

The teen years are already a time of change and struggle and growth. When you add in these ever-mounting pressures and expectations, you get kids that are overstressed, overworked, overloaded, and overwhelmed.

And, this isn't just my opinion. The really smart science-y people have studied this very thing and what they're finding is quite honestly, concerning.

Remember the stress response we talked about earlier? You know, the "fight or flight" response that saved our ancestors from being a dinosaur snack? It turns out that during the teen years, this stress response is still forming and maturing. What that means is teens are often more sensitive to stressors than adults. Studies have found that prolonged, chronic stress causes changes in the teen brain that can take a long time to repair. Prolonged stress has been linked to issues like higher levels of anxiety, depression, and other mental health issues.

A 2018 survey by the American Psychological Association found that teens report higher levels of stress than adults. They are the most likely of all generations to report poor mental health. They are also more likely to see professional help for their issues.

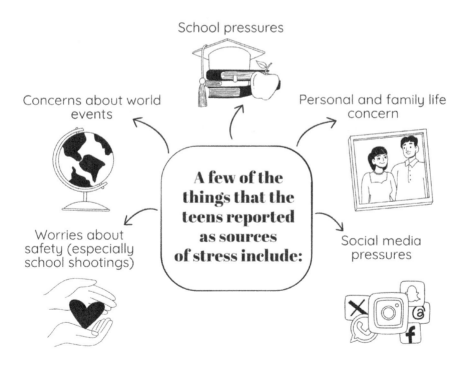

School pressures

Concerns about world events

Personal and family life concern

A few of the things that the teens reported as sources of stress include:

Worries about safety (especially school shootings)

Social media pressures

And, the stress on teens is increasing. According to a 2019 study, between 2005 and 2017, serious psychological distress, major depression, and suicide risks are on the rise for teens and young adults.

So I won't bore you with tons of statistics but you get the point: Teens are stressed out.

Think about your own life. What kinds of things are stressing you out? What are your biggest worries?

Right about now, you're probably thinking, "Everybody gets stressed out. That's life. What can you do about it?"

That's a great question and I am about to give you some answers.

Ways You Can Manage Your Stress

First, you need to know this:

You CAN manage your stress and anxiety. You're smart. You're resourceful. You may not know it yet, but you already have the strength inside you to handle things like a BOSS. Stress makes us anxious and remember what I told you about anxiety? Anxiety is a liar and wants you to believe that you can't do hard things. Guess what? I'm here to tell you that you *can*.

Managing stress is different than making stress go away. I wish I could tell you that you could make it all go away but life doesn't work that way.

What you can do is learn some ways to 1) let go of worrying about what you cannot control or change (there's a lot of that, even for grown-ups). 2) find healthy ways to cope with and either eliminate or manage the stressors you can do something about, and 3) recognize when you need help and ask for it. (This last one is super hard, even for grown grown-ups. At some point, you have to choose a path for once you're out of school. You have to follow the law. You get the idea. Sometimes in life, there are just things we do because they're part of being a productive member of your community and they help prepare you for adulthood.

Sometimes I hear people say, "No I don't have to. I just won't do it." News flash: not choosing is still a choice you make. Now, sometimes, yes. You may find yourself in a situation that is just not ok or safe in some way. You may have to make the choice to say no or walk away. If you find yourself there, ask yourself whether you're saying no because it really is not safe or healthy, or whether you're just mad you can't have your way. Every choice has a consequence. Good or bad. It's up to you to choose.

Accepting What Is

You've heard the saying, "It is what it is." Sometimes, it's these things we cannot control or change that we let stress us the most. One of the ways to deal with things we cannot change is by practicing something called acceptance. It's the ability to accept that some things are not within our power or control to change. Instead of stressing over what just is, what if you could let it roll on past you? The idea is to not waste energy on what just is. You can't change it, so you change how you react to it.

Here's an example: Your parents say homework done before you take the car out. It's not negotiable. (It wasn't negotiable in my house either.) Now, you could throw a wild-eyed fit. I'm betting it would end with something like no car, no car keys, and everybody's mad. Depending on how out of the box you got, you might even be grounded for some time.

A better way to handle a situation might be to decide, "OK, I know the rule. I don't like it but I can't change it. So, my choices are, throw a fit and see if they cave (unlikely) or just do my homework so I can bounce." Hmm...I know what I'd choose. Stuck home when all my friends are out sucks. Sometimes, the smarter (sometimes harder) decision is to just do what needs to be done and be done with it.

Now, I can't lie. Learning to practice acceptance takes practice. We all live in a "right now" kind of world. We expect to get what we want, how we want, when we want it. But it doesn't always work that way. Pushing against what you can't change or get right now is just stressful. Stop stressing yourself out.

Acceptance can work with rules you have to follow, feelings you have, situations you find yourself in...all kinds of things. Learn to recognize when acceptance is a healthy choice.

Think of some things you can't change but you keep trying to push those limits and getting stressed out. What are some ways to approach them with acceptance?

Dealing With Your Stress

Life is full of everyday stressors: school, friends, relationships, parents, homework, exams...the list goes on. You can't eliminate stress entirely but there are things you can do to lessen it and/or cope with it in healthy ways.

For example, school is stressful, right? Well, you can't make it go away but you can learn ways to relax and to cope with the stress.

When we talk about stress management, we're talking about coping: finding strategies or activities that help to bring down the anxiety, worry, and tension while increasing feelings of relaxation and calm.

One thing we know about the brain and the body is that it needs time to relax. It's during these times of relaxation that the body and brain are replenishing their energy and getting ready for what comes next. For example, did you know that while you're sleeping, the brain is working to refresh itself, storing your memories and what you learned that day, and energizing itself for the next day? That's why parents are always on you to get your sleep. When your brain is well-rested, it functions better, you recall information better, and, here's a big one, your mood is more stable.

Before we talk about specific things you can do to manage stress, I want to tell you about one of the most powerful things I ever found to help me with managing my world. It goes along with all of the specific strategies I am going to tell you about. You might have heard of this before, maybe not. That power-house is called mindfulness.

The Power of Mindfulness

I started with this chapter with acceptance because I want you to get in the habit of seeing things as they are, not the way you want them to be or worry that they might be or wish they were. Accepting where you are, right now, dealing with where you are, *right now*, is the key to managing stress. This is what being mindful is all about. It's the life cheat code you've probably never heard that holds all the power when it comes to dealing with the things that stress you out.

So what exactly is mindfulness?

There are lots of ways to describe mindfulness, but they all basically mean the same thing: Mindfulness, or being mindful, means that your mind is fully attuned to what's happening in the moment, what you're doing, thinking, and feeling, and to your surroundings. Another way to describe it is being in the moment or in the "here-and-now". Mindfulness can also be a specific way of learning to think that can help with stress reduction, anxiety management, and other issues.

Mindfulness can sound like some silly way of thinking but it's actually a way of thinking that you probably use more than you think.

- Focusing on something you're really, really interested in, like drawing or fixing your bike. Your whole attention is right there. Mindful.

- You're deep into a conversation with your best friend and you're listening to every word. Nothing else has your attention. Mindful.

- Taking your chemistry test and you're 100% focused on your exam. Nothing is distracting you. Mindful.

So, mindfulness or being mindful is not some magical, mysterious thing. We do it naturally. We shift in and out of being focused and attentive many times a day.

Now, the problem comes in when you have a gazillion things competing for your attention and your mind is wandering more than it's focusing. It's harder to get things done. You get stressed out. It can be overwhelming. They've actually studied this phenomenon and found that people who are more mindful are more likely to report higher levels of happiness. Not surprisingly, mindfulness is at the heart of a lot of philosophical and religious traditions that teach that happiness is to be found by living in the moment. As the researchers put it, "These traditions suggest that a wandering mind is an unhappy mind."

Because it is such a powerful influence on happiness and well-being, the practice of mindfulness has also found its way in the health and mental health world. People have found that being more mindful helps them to feel calmer and less anxious. It has been shown to reduce worry, improve mood, improve focus and memory, and more.

You might even be familiar with some of the ways people learn better mindfulness. Activities like yoga, Tai Chi, and meditation are just a few that incorporate mindfulness into their practice.

FUN FACT: You can make brushing your teeth a more mindful activity simply by focusing intently on what you're doing. 100% true.

Now, why am I telling you all this? Because practicing mindfulness is quite simply, a game-changer. It can help you to focus on the now and worry less about the "what ifs". It can help you take control of your emotions and live in a more calm, focused way. When you're focused on now, there's no room for worry. Game. Changer.

So, I want to share just a few of my favorite mindfulness activities that have helped me so much over the years. You've probably heard of some of them. You might have even tried some of them before.

I would encourage you to try a few of them out and see what you like. The cool thing is that there are a gazillion ways to practice mindfulness and no right or wrong.

What's the best way? The way that works for you.

Mindful Breathing

Mindful breathing, sometimes referred to as "breathwork", is similar to the breathing techniques we talked about earlier. They have an element of mindfulness too in that you're paying attention to your breathing pattern.

★ Start by sitting or lying down in a comfortable position. Some people like to close their eyes. It's up to you. I close mine so I don't get distracted.

★ Next, take a deep breath, inhaling through the nose, feeling your stomach expand. You can gently place your hand over your belly if it helps you focus.

★ Slowly breathe out through your mouth.

★ Do this a few times and notice that you're settling into a pattern of normal breathing. What that pattern is, is unique to you.

★ Continue to breathe, noticing the rise and fall of your belly as you breathe.

★ You may hear noises around you. Thoughts may enter your awareness. That's ok. Notice that they are there. With no judgment, mentally brush them aside gently and continue focusing on your breathing.

★ Continue breathing until you feel calm and relaxed. Notice how your mind and body feel.

★ Be sure to get up slowly.

Mindful breathing is a bit different in that it is less structured. You're not counting. You're simply paying attention, being mindful, of your breathing. Mindfulness here is used to help you focus on your experience right now, in the moment. Here-and-now.

Take 5 or 10 minutes each day to practice.

Have you ever done any breathwork? If so, what was it like for you? If not, is this something you'd consider trying? Why or why not?

Journaling

OK now, before you think "Oh great. Writing and homework", hear me out. This is not your parents' journaling and it certainly isn't your English class journaling.

Journaling is nothing more than taking your thoughts and putting them on paper. So, what's mindful about this? When you journal, you are focusing your attention on your inner thoughts. You are exploring thoughts you might not have been aware of before. Or, you might focus on thoughts that are pleasant, bothersome, or just neutral. Remember, thoughts influence behavior so understanding those thoughts can give you clarity and help you sort things out.

So why journaling? Journaling has been shown to reduce stress, manage anxiety, and helps to improve mood. All from writing? Yes!

Journaling:

★ Helps you to clear your head, sort of problems and fears

★ Allows you to recognize patterns of thinking and behavior, like triggers, giving you insight into possible solutions

★ Gives you a place for positive self-talk and recognizing your accomplishments

One of my favorite journaling activities is the Brain Dump. It's a great strategy for when you've got tons of thoughts just swirling around in your head. Take out your journal and just write. No structure. No certain form. Just write until you feel your thoughts start to settle down and you begin to feel relief. It might be 2 minutes. It might take 5 or 10 or more.

Have you journaled before? How was that experience for you? If you haven't journaled before, what are you most curious about with the process of journaling?

If you feel ready, I invite you to start a journaling practice. If you're stuck with how to start, check out the list of Journaling

Prompts at the end of the book. These prompts can get you started until you feel ready to use your own ideas.

Moments of Stillness

I know, that sounds funny but the fact is, stillness is a powerful thing. Our brains are full of chatter all day long, taking in information, processing information, and deciding what to do, all the while keeping us alive and breathing. We are constantly in motion. All that noise and movement can make you anxious and leave you feeling overloaded.

Moments of stillness are tiny moments you can take any time you need a "mini-break". These breaks give your brain a break from that constant stimulation. They also help your body to relax and promote mindfulness.

Here's a simple idea for a "taking a moment":

Take a moment, find a quiet place where you can sit quietly and be still. You may hear some noise around you. Try to mentally brush it aside as you focus on being still. Allow yourself to sit quietly for a few minutes. Notice how your body and mind respond.

Practicing Gratitude

Huh? Yes. Believe it or not, being grateful has POWERFUL effects on your well-being and sense of self. But what is gratitude exactly?

Gratitude is more than just saying thank you to people. Gratitude is a more expansive feeling of thankfulness or gratefulness for kindness, help, support, and other kinds of generosity we might receive from others. Gratitude can even extend to your world.

Really smart people have discovered that feeling grateful does awesome things for our sense of well-being. Studies have found that being grateful, what they call practicing gratitude, can improve sleep, reduce stress, improve mood and even help with relationships. There's even some evidence that it can have a positive effect on health too. Practicing gratitude helps you focus on the positive which in turn leads to a positive outlook and attitude. And, positivity is contagious!!

How to Start A Gratitude Practice

Practicing gratitude doesn't have to be complicated. One simple, but very effective, way to practice gratitude is the **3 Good Things** Today activity.

Each day (choose to do this morning or evening), write down 3 positives or "good" things that happened that day and why they were positive for you.

Do this each day over the course of a week. At the end of the week, reflect on your blessings for that week.

Many people practice gratitude as an ongoing activity. It's up to you. You may find that it's a positive way to start or end your day.

To get you started, I've included a *3 Good Things Today* template at the end of the book for you to use.

Now It's Your Turn

Choose one or more mindfulness practices to try. Keep track of how it makes you feel. Which ones will you choose to continue? Which ones will you discard?

Choose at least one practice to continue. Track your response over time, paying attention to your mood, anxiety, sleep, and other factors that are important to you.

Conclusion

Well, my friend, we've come to the end of our time together. I have enjoyed sharing some of my journey with you. I hope that you have learned some things that you will find helpful as you move towards adulthood.

Before we finish our time here, I want to encourage you to continue working to have the life you want. We, as humans, are always a work in progress. And, what's awesome is that every day, every minute, every breath is a reminder that you're still here and a chance to start over.

So, I shared a lot of my experience with you. How did it end for me?

Well, with some help from a counselor and my family, reading some great self-help books, and a lot of me working on myself, I made it through my teen years. Sure, I made some mistakes along the way. We all do. I learned so much about myself. I entered adulthood feeling more confident that I have the skills to make good choices and live the life I want. Now, I will say that self-improvement and self-care is a journey. We are constantly growing and changing. I still practice a lot of the skills I shared with you like journaling, mindfulness, stress management, and relaxation. I seek support when I need it because life has a way of surprising us and sometimes, we need help figuring it out.

Let yourself be open to growth and you will find the path that is meant for you. It might not be the one you envision today, and that's ok. Focus on taking care of yourself and your path will open before you.

I'd like to leave you with a final thought. This quote from Will Smith sums up the power of hope simply and beautifully:

"I wake up every morning believing today is going to be better than yesterday."

I hope that you will start each day this way and continue to learn and grow. You are going to amaze yourself at what you will accomplish. There's a whole world waiting for you.

If You Need Help

If you find yourself with more questions...

If you find yourself struggling with your feelings...

If you find yourself wanting to talk to someone...

This section is for you.

Sometimes you need more than a BFF or a parent. Sometimes, you need someone who can be objective while still being supportive. Someone who will tell you what you NEED to hear and not just what you want to hear. Someone who can help you sort through all the thoughts and feelings and find the solutions that make sense for you.

We've talked about a lot of topics and explored a lot of areas of your life that you might not have looked at before. You may be left with questions or wanting to know more about some aspect.

In this section, I have assembled some of what I consider the best resources out there for teens to learn more about mental health topics or to find help. I've included resources for finding a therapist, for relaxation and wellness, for learning more about mental health topics, and even resources for talking to someone if you're feeling like you want to talk to someone right away.

Before we look at the list, let me say this: Sometimes, people experience very intense and painful feelings, leaving them feeling unsafe or unable to maintain their own safety. It doesn't mean that you are "bad" or "broken" or "wrong". It simply means that you're dealing with feelings that are bigger than what you might be prepared to handle. It can happen to teens and it can happen to adults too. If you find yourself having thoughts of harming yourself, or if your friend is feeling that way, there is *immediate* help. If you're feeling unsafe, you can always tell a trusted adult, call 911 or go to your nearest emergency room and they will help you. There is no shame in asking for help and they will know how to help you get through that difficult time safely.

Find A Therapist

+ **National Board for Certified Counselors Counselor Find**
  https://www.nbcc.org/search/counselorfind

+ **Psychology Today Therapist Directory**
  https://www.psychologytoday.com/us/therapists

+ **American Psychological Association**
  https://locator.apa.org/

+ **American Association of Marriage & Family Therapists Find A Therapist**
  https://aamft.org/Directories/Find_a_Therapist.aspx

+ **TalkSpace (online therapy)**
  https://www.talkspace.com/

National Suicide Prevention Lifeline

 Voice **1-800-273-8255**

Text HOME to **741741**
from anywhere in the United States, anytime.

Apps for Relaxation

These apps are available in the App Store and Google Play Store

- ✦ Calm
- ✦ Oak
- ✦ Headspace
- ✦ Medito
- ✦ Waking Up

Helpful Websites

- ✦ **National Institute of Mental Health**
  https://www.nimh.nih.gov

- ✦ **PsyCom**
  https://www.psycom.net/

- ✦ **WebMD Mental Health Center**
  https://www.webmd.com/mental-health/default.htm

- ✦ **Psychology Today**
  https://www.psychologytoday.com/us

- ✦ **American Institute of Stress**
  https://www.stress.org/

- ✦ **Mayo Clinic Anxiety Coach**
  https://anxietycoach.mayoclinic.org/anxiety/

Suggestions For Parents

O K first, to the teens reading so far...

So, I know you're going to read this and say, "Hey why are we getting mom and dad involved here? Isn't this for me?"

First, yes, this book is written for you. However, chances are, your parent either bought the book for you or you live at home, maybe both. Either way, your parents are most likely in your life.

Second, your parents are most likely in your life. Yes, I said that twice because it's easy to get into the mindset of "I'm grown" or "I can make my own decisions" and "It's not their business" and the like. While some of that is debatable, I get it. Teens generally don't like to share a lot with grown-ups and especially their parents.

However, if you're serious about making positive changes in your life, you need your parents to support you. You need their guidance, even if it doesn't always feel that way. Remember I told you in the beginning they had insight that you couldn't possibly have yet? This is where it matters most.

And, the most important reason for including your parents in this process is because if you are going to be doing things differently, they need to understand what you're doing and how they can support you. Why?

First off, because someone, especially someone's child, does something new, good or not, it is unexpected and gets attention. Everyone turns their attention to them as in, "What the heck is going on here?" "Who are you and what did you do with my kid?" You're not necessarily doing anything wrong. They are just trying to figure out what you're up to.

Here's an example: Say that whenever you and your dad disagree, it usually ends with you being mad and storming off. The issue never gets resolved, everyone is mad, and you feel like he didn't hear what you were trying to say. You've played this out a million times. Now, say instead of getting mad and storming off, you decide to use those good communication skills you've learned:

"Dad, I feel nervous when you raise your voice because I don't know what to say. I would really like to be able to talk to each other even when we don't agree."

The first time you do that, your dad will probably stop and scratch his head like, huh? "What just happened here?" He's expecting you to storm off but instead, you're trying to communicate with him.

Chances are when that happens, you'll see him calm down and that's the second why of why involving parents matters. As you do things differently, your parents will do so too. Not because you're "making" them or "demanding" them to. Rather, you're seeing human behavior in action. When one person does something different, it changes the pattern and allows the other person to respond differently too.

I mean, think about it: how funny would your dad look if you calmly used your "I feel..." and instead of stopping to hear you, he continued arguing? Yeah, he'd look foolish. Doing something different gives everyone a chance to step back and take a breath. And listen.

So, that's why we want parents involved. Because you need them to understand what you're trying to do. They may not agree with every single choice you make and that's ok. They don't have to. It's their job to guide you and keep you from going off into the ditch. You want them to understand what you're trying to do and support you when you're making healthy choices. And call you out when you're headed towards the ditch. But when they don't understand what you're doing, it scares them. Let them guide you. Let them support you. And, let them understand you.

OK, that's it for you, teen reader, for now. There are no secrets here. This part is to help mom and dad understand what you're trying to do.

The rest of this chapter is for moms and dads.

HELLO MOMS AND DADS!

I'm so glad you've chosen to share in your teen's quest to improve their coping skills and life strategies. As you well know, the teen years are chock full of ups and downs, victories and losses, sweet successes along with trials, and tribulations. Add in the hormonal ups and downs and you have a never-ending rollercoaster for even the most well-adjusted teen. Sometimes all those who love them can do is hang on tight!

Connecting with your teen can be hard on a good day. Some days, it can seem like you're talking to a closed door. Keep trying! Every now and then, they'll crack that door just a tiny bit and give you a glimpse inside.

You love them and they know you do. But, teens and parents often speak different languages. A lot of arguments happen because you're just not connecting, even though you might be talking about the same thing! It is enough to drive you nuts!

The truth is, most kids want to talk to their parents but in *their own* way. There's an interesting approach for connecting with someone that you've probably heard before in some form: meet people where they are and not where you expect them to be. Teens speak their own language. Engage with them in ways that they know how to engage in *now* and not necessarily the way they *should be* engaging or *will be* someday. How they *should be* communicating may not even be in their skill set yet. With patience and guidance, it will come.

Now, this isn't a free pass for them to be ugly or disrespectful. That's never ok and is a whole different issue requiring a different response. What I'm talking about is making a connection with them in a way that encourages communication and lets them learn that it's safe to express themselves to you and that it can be satisfying too. They also learn that every conversation doesn't have to be what they didn't do or a talk about consequences. Sometimes, it can be nice just to have a chat. That is a *powerful* foundation to build on.

Expect that in the beginning, your teen might just be a little suspicious of your new approach. After all, they're expecting the same old set up that ends in a stalemate. Keep going and be patient. When they see you're seeking to understand and not battle, an amazing thing happens – you start listening to each other, and the dynamic shifts.

Before I share my tips with you, let me share the caveat that I've heard from every mental health resource I've ever read: your role is a parent, not a friend. Not that you can't have fun together but you're raising an adult. There will be time for you to be friends. Right now, they need you to parent and guide them safely to adulthood.

When you treat a child as a peer, it sets you both up to fail. Friends implies that nobody is "in charge". Friends share in our shenanigans and do the fun things with us. Friends are our confidantes. They don't set rules and limits or discipline us. Friends don't tell us to clean our rooms or go to school or ground us when we've done something wrong. And there's more.

Research has shown that kids do better when their parents show love and affection and still enforce age-appropriate limits. More permissive parenting styles have been linked with poor self-control in children.

We are going to talk a lot about talking to your teen. Having a good rapport is important for your teen. Teens who have a healthy, meaningful rapport with their parents tend to have higher-quality relationships and lower rates of delinquency. Of course, it's important to be sure those conversations are healthy and age-appropriate. As close as you and your teen might be, it's important to avoid sharing things that you'd share with a confidante and maintain that parent-child boundary.

I'd like to share some ideas for supporting your teen that might help to break down those walls that they seem to throw up when things get uncomfortable. Some of these suggestions are things I wish someone had shared with my parents. They were awesome parents, but I don't think they always knew how to help me. Some of these other suggestions come from things I learned about on my own journey of healing. Just as I've said to your teen, not every strategy works for every person. Try different ways of approaching and see what works best for the two of you.

Listen Often

Every day, your teen is sharing information. Are you listening? They're not likely to come up and say, "Hey mom, guess what...." They ARE likely to talk about something seemingly benign to you but important in their world. When they share something, ANYTHING, listen to what is being said. It might be a casual comment about something on social media or a song they heard or something about school. Listen.

Those seemingly benign comments can be a glimpse into what's happening in their world. Sometimes, those remarks are testing the water to see if you're open to hearing more. Now, it might just be about a social media post or a song or school. Other times, it might be an opportunity to connect. Just listen.

The takeaway here is that your kid is cracking that door open. In this moment, *you* are the person they want to engage with. How you respond sends a powerful message about whether you're interested, if they can trust you with their feelings and the likelihood that they will come to you with the really big things. Sometimes, their comment is telling you about the important thing. *Listen.*

How well do you think you listen to your teen? Do you think they would agree?

No Judgement Zone

Sharing feelings is one of the hardest things for a person to do. For teens, especially those who might be dealing with self-esteem or anxiety, or confidence, it can be especially hard. Expressing feelings requires someone to be vulnerable and open themselves to how others might respond. That's a pretty scary thought when you're not feeling sure of yourself.

One thing to keep in mind (and it's hard) is that feelings are highly personal. They are not right or wrong. We simply feel what we feel and it doesn't always make sense to ourselves, much less to someone else. Teens can really struggle with feelings. They're growing and learning so many things so quickly that it can take some time to sort it all out. When they tell you they don't know how they feel, they're probably telling you the truth. Listen and look deeper.

If your teen feels safe enough to share their feelings with you, any feelings, the most important response you can give is validation, something that lets them know, "I hear you." How you respond sends a powerful message of whether or not it is emotion-
ally safe to share their feelings with you: "Can I say how I feel without you judging me or telling me why I'm wrong or why I shouldn't feel that way?"

Now, you may not understand why your teen feels the way they do and you might even disagree with them. That's ok. You don't have to. They might not understand yours either. Simply acknowledging their feelings is all that is needed.

And sometimes, it opens the door for a deeper conversation: "Would you like to talk about that?" They might not always say yes but trust and self-confidence build over time. When a teen feels heard and respected, they're more likely to share again. Be ready.

How do you let your teen know, "I hear you"?

Trust: The Secret Sauce

Trust is the thing that makes ALL the difference with teens. If they know they can trust you, you're halfway there.

For most teens, trust and respect are hard to earn and harder to keep. It requires a good deal of trust for a teen to share sometimes very personal things. When your teen tells you something in confidence, it is important to respect the trust being placed with you and not share it with others.

A common example where this gets things in the ditch is with families. Your kid tells you something in confidence and you later casually mention it to a sibling. Uh oh. Now your kid doesn't trust you and their sibling knows something that they didn't want to share with them. Siblings often use each other's pain points as ammunition to get on each other's nerves. You've been given an important piece of their personal life to guard.

Now, this isn't the typical "Dad, don't tell mom" or "Mom, don't tell Dad." That's a triangle you don't want to be in. I'm talking about when your teen shares something personal with you, especially if you know it was hard for them to open up. Be respectful of their feelings. Each time your teen places trust in you and you honor that trust, it's more likely that they will come to you again. Violate this trust and they will 100% not share again anytime soon. And you don't want that. There will be big things that happen that you hope your kid will talk to you about.

Sometimes kids share things that to grown ups seem insignificant. To your kid, though, it could be the most embarrassing thing ever. If you aren't sure if it's ok to share, ask. Of course, you want to use the "need to know" rule. Before you share something your teen has shared, ask yourself, "does this person *need* to know?" Kids are pretty reasonable if they know you are trying to respect them.

For example, your teen might be OK with you telling the other parent but not grandma, the neighbor, and three cousins. Better yet, your teen might want to be the one to tell the other parent. If your child requests confidentiality, provide it if at all possible.

If it's a situation where you can't promise to keep their confidence, let them know that and why. Together you can decide what to do. This is where all the time you've spent building trust and communication REALLY pays off. If your teen knows that you can be trusted and that you have their best interest at heart, they are much more likely to handle the situation with you. Will they be happy about it? Zero chance of that. What they will be happy about is that you didn't disrespect them or betray their trust. That is everything.

What do you think is the current trust level between you and your teen? Do you think they would agree? Is there something you can do to strengthen that bond?

Keep Your Cool

This one is the challenge of every parent. Your teen is going to do things that will work your very last nerve and want to ground them for life...after you're done yelling at them for an hour. At the same time, you adore them.

At some point, your teen may come to you with, or you may discover, something big. This is the time to take a deep breath and choose your response carefully. In the heat of the moment, we tend to say and do things we might not say or do in a calmer moment. Sometimes those words and actions hurt without intending to. Or don't do anything to support your teen.

How you respond lets them know if it is safe to continue engaging with you. They may take your response personally, and assume your reaction is about them, even if it isn't. If your teen thinks you are about to go off or feels harshly judged, it's almost guaranteed the conversation will be over before it starts.

If you have a teen who's struggling with things like self-esteem, or communication, or anxiety, coming to you is hard. They're sensitive to the reactions of others. They want and need support but asking can be so hard. Your teen is looking for guidance, support, and maybe safety or protection. What you hear might freak you out. That's ok, and it's ok to say so. At the same time, your teen needs to know that you are in control. When you're calm, they're calm. Just breathe.

You are your teen's soft place to fall. You've got them.

Offer Your Support

You might have bought this book for your teen hoping to find some help and guidance for them. Or, they bought it and have probably shared it with you. Either way,  here you are. Your teen is seeking knowledge and seeking your support. If they've shared the book with you, they are offering you a glimpse into their world.

Adopt an open-door policy. Let them know that you are open to any conversation and will listen without judgment. Let them know you are there when they are ready.

Encourage Them To Try

One of the things I say often is that anxiety lies. It convinces us that we can't do something, that others will judge, that we will fail. Kids who tend to be anxious or lack self-confidence struggle with facing that fear. It's easier to retreat, avoid, and isolate.

It's not likely that they will seek out opportunities to try on their own, at least in the beginning.

As your teen starts to share a little bit with you about what they're trying to work on, be mindful of opportunities that might come along for them to engage or practice what they're trying to learn. For example, maybe your teen is trying to be more socially engaged but is hesitant to venture out on his or her own. Look for opportunities for them to get out and do something with a peer or a sibling, cousin, or friend. Something relatively simple might be to create an opportunity for them to invite a friend to see a movie or grab a coffee. Something simple and familiar but not overwhelming. Of course, this is an example. Your teen may have other interests you might be able to support.

Be careful not to push or make it feel like a "demand" or "work". Your teen will already be nervous and that anxiety is whispering those words of "don't do it" in their ear. Support and encourage. And offer lots of praise when they succeed. It isn't always easy to see our own behavior and whether we've succeeded or not.

Praise, Praise, Praise

There's an old saying that for every negative, it takes 10 positives to overcome. In other words, for every criticism or negative remark, a person needs 10 times the positive feedback to feel good about what happened. We all need praise and positive feedback. Kids who deal with low self-esteem, low confidence, anxiety, and such are super sensitive to criticism, teasing (even good-hearted joking), or judgment. Compliments and positive feedback make us feel good and send the message that, "Hey, I did something right!" When we get positive feedback, it also creates a pleasurable memory and makes it more likely that they will do it again, and maybe more.

A few ways to offer positive feedback or praise is to focus on the behavior you see. For example,

- If you see them really trying, but not quite there yet, compliment their step in the right direction. They may not be able to see their progress yet.

- If you see them making an effort, let them know that you see how hard they're working.

- If they achieve something that is really hard for them (even if it seems minor to you), offer praise and positive feedback.

- Catch them doing it right. This is an old parenting trick that works with people in general. Praise and compliments are among the most powerful behavior changers. Focus on the action. For example, if you know they are working on assertiveness: "I really like the way that you told me how you feel about..."

Now, all this positive feedback and praise doesn't mean that there won't be times you will need to offer constructive criticism. You will. And they will need it. The key to delivering that kind of feedback is to lead with kindness.

Giving your teen feedback allows them the opportunity to grow and change. It also allows you to take on the role of a guide as opposed to a disciplinarian. These opportunities are teachable moments.

- Point out what your teen did well. Offer suggestions for what he or she could do better next time. Constructive feedback is you offering your opinion and advice as someone with experience your teen doesn't have yet. It's not the time for discussing broken rules or bad behavior. Gently suggesting that they put shoes on before leaving for school is constructive feedback. Taking their electronics for not getting homework done is giving consequences.

- Be kind. Be mindful of body language and voice tone. You want your teen to feel that you're approachable and that this isn't going to turn into a "lecture". You already know how that ends.

- Use I-statements. This is a skill your teen will understand. I-statements allow you to say how you feel and what you think directly. For more about I-statements, check out Chapter 2 on Communication.

A few Don'ts here:

- Avoid comparing your teen to others, especially a sibling. They already know their shortcomings or struggles. They've probably compared themselves already.

- Avoid the "yeah buts". These statements, while often well-intentioned, get interpreted as negative feedback. For example, say getting homework done is always a battle.

Kid: "Hey mom (or dad), my homework is done."

Parent: "Yeah, I'm glad you got your homework done today, but I wish you'd do that every day."

Put another way:

Kid: "Hey mom (or dad), my homework is done."

Parent: "I'm glad you got your homework done today. Good job."

Hear the difference? Your teen is more likely to hear the first response as negative criticism and the "I can't do anything right." Focus on the behavior at hand. You'll give the message you intend and you're more likely to avoid either a skirmish or a teen who just stops listening.

Ask for Help

Just like I tell teens, there is no shame in asking for help. None of us know everything and that goes for adults too. Kids aren't born with an owner's manual. Parents do the best they can. Sometimes kids need help that parents can't give them.

If you find that you're struggling with parenting, or just figuring out how to support your teen, there are awesome parenting resources and family therapists who can help. Sometimes having a fresh perspective can shed light on some different ways of approaching a problem.

If you see that your teen is still struggling despite trying the self-help route and support from you, there might be some bigger issues to address. There are therapists who specialize in teen issues who can really help.

I tried everything I knew to do until I couldn't do it anymore. Reaching out for help was one of the best decisions I could have made. I only wondered why I hadn't done it sooner.

If you're looking for resources, I have included a resources section that includes additional reading suggestions, finding a therapist and more.

Thank you for being the safe harbor for your teen. They need you even when they don't know they need you. You're doing great.

Useful Templates and Tools

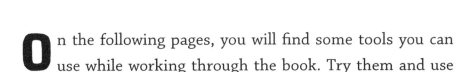

O n the following pages, you will find some tools you can use while working through the book. Try them and use what works best for you!

- Quick Guide to Setting Personal Goals

- SMART Goals Template

- Steps to Success Ladder

- Social Media Plan Template

- 3 Good Things Today

- Feelings Wheel

- Journaling Prompts

- Thought Challenge Template

QUICK GUIDE TO SETTING PERSONAL GOALS

Since you're reading this book, you've probably decided that it is time to make some changes in your life. Maybe you're trying to feel more positive and confident. Maybe you're trying to figure out how to be more outgoing or make friends more easily. Maybe it's something else entirely.

Whatever it is, one thing is true: change takes work. You can wish and hope and dream. You can have all the best and biggest plans in the world. Maybe you've tried to get there but just can't seem to figure it out. After too much trying, you might feel like you're just stuck in neutral, wondering if what you're trying to change is even worth it.

Sound familiar? If so, you're not alone.

Albert Einstein famously said that insanity is "doing the same thing over and over again and expecting different results." In other words, continuing to do what doesn't work and hoping one day you magically have what you want gets you nowhere but stuck where you are. Makes no sense right?

Wishing and hoping doesn't get you where you want to go. It just gets you more frustrated.

Change is hard work. When we are trying to make a change, we usually start by looking around to see what other people are doing. And, maybe this isn't the first book you're reading looking for help. What lots of people, including me, have found is that everyone you ask has the BEST idea for getting what you want. Lots of resources tell you their way is the BEST. Well, let me just say that if all it took to make changes in my life was to ask somebody or just do what somebody told me to, then I wasted a ton of time and money. I could have just had someone say, "Do it the way I did Forrest" or "Just do what I say." Yeah, that didn't work.

Why? The problem there is actually two issues. First, their ways worked for them. I am not them. You are not them and you are not me. Telling someone to "just do this" doesn't consider who you are as a person, what you like, what your strengths are, and what you need. Second, and this is the secret sauce, just telling you something doesn't help you to set goals. Goals are a specific way of getting yourself from point A to point B. And not just any goals. SMART Goals are the secret sauce of successful change.

SMART GOALS

It's easy to think you can read a book, watch a video or just hope and get what you want. You might even make a sort of plan. Now, all those things can help you get information, but they all lack one thing: Action.

Here's the 411 on change: you have to DO SOMETHING. **YOU NEED A PLAN OF ACTION.**

SMART goals are more than just a vague idea of what you want to do. SMART goals are goals that are written in a very specific way using a very specific format that has been proven to improve your chances of getting what you want.

So, what's a SMART Goal look like?

SMART goals consist of five specific elements. Each one defines a piece of the plan that, when put together, defines what you're working on and exactly what you need to do to get there. A SMART goal will also tell you when you've reached your goal. After all, if you don't know what you're working towards, how would you know when you get there?

When you get ready to write your goal, remember this acronym: S.M.A.R.T.

S	Specific
M	Measurable
A	Achievable
R	Relevant
T	Time-limited

S: Specific means that your goal is very detailed and clear.

What *exactly* do I want to achieve? What would that look like to me? What steps will you take?

M: Measurable means that you have a way to assess your progress.

For example, if your goal is to be able to ask someone out on a date, you need to have a way to measure the steps you'll take.

- Did you say hi? Check.

- Did you introduce yourself? Check.

- Did you have a conversation with this person? Check.

- And so on until you reach the step of asking someone out.

The measurement you use depends on your goal. You want to use a unit of measure that you can track.

A: Achievable means that your goals are realistically reachable. In other words, you have to keep it real here. We ALL have limitations and there are just some things we can't do. For example, I'm an average height, dark-haired guy. I will never be a 6-foot tall, blonde bikini model. Your goals should be challenging and move you out of your comfort zone but still within your range of abilities and resources. Otherwise, you set yourself up to fail.

R: Relevant means that your goal *means something to you*. Let's be real, people don't commit to or really put effort into things that don't have meaning for them. Choose to work on things that are important to you and relevant to your life and situation. It can be tempting to do things because your friends are doing it or your parents want you to or you want to impress someone. Do it for you.

T: Time-Limited means that your goal has a clear ending point. You don't just do something until. At the end of the time, evaluate where you are. You might need to reset your goal or you may have achieved it and are ready for the next step. A good goal never leaves you wondering.

Why SMART Goals Matter

Just thinking about something, even wishing for it 24/7, doesn't make it so. You have to get your head in the right space too. Specific and detailed goals puts you in a mindset that is focused on success:

- When you write your goals down, you're setting an intention and committing to doing the work.

- Specific, well-thought-out goals define *exactly* what you're working towards.

- Setting your own goal helps you to feel in control of your direction and your progress.

- Seeing your progress boosts confidence and motivates you to keep going!

So, why am I spending time telling you about goals and not talking about social skills? Because in order for you to make the changes you want to make, you need to set goals for yourself. This is one area I WISH someone had told me about. I spent so much time flailing around trying to find my way and always wondering why I was stuck in the same place. I had ideas of what I wanted and did all kinds of things like reading self-help books and talking to people. But, I had no action plan. Once I discovered how to set goals and get myself moving in the right direction, it was a game-changer!

Now, getting started with thinking in this way takes practice. I have included some templates to help you practice writing your goals in a more action-focused way. Don't worry if they are not perfect. They don't have to be. The important thing is that you are setting your intentions and plan in place. You can then start to take steps – the action part that so many people miss!

Now It's Your Turn

Abraham Lincoln once said, "A goal properly set is halfway reached." Deciding what you want to achieve is the first step.

Take a piece of paper and write down what you think your goal is. It might take a bit of writing to get it out and narrowed down to something you feel is specific enough. You can start anywhere on the page. You can just write. Maybe you prefer to make a list or even doodle a picture. Whatever works for you is ok. Just continue to write until you feel like you've gotten to your goal.

Here are some questions to help you if you need help getting started:

The goal I want to work on now is:

- What could get in the way of achieving my goal?

- What can I do to avoid or eliminate these obstacles?

- What will I need to reach my goals? (Resources, finances, education, support, etc.)

- Who can help me reach my goals? (List family members, friends, teachers, or others who can help you meet your goals)

My Timeline

- Goal –

- Kickoff Date –

- Target Date –

At the end of this section, you will find a SMART Goals form that you can use to record your goals.

One final thing about goals and changing behavior: change takes time. Sometimes a lot of time. It's been said that a new habit is formed in 21 days. That may be true for some behaviors. Other changes can take much longer.

When you are trying to change a behavior, you're replacing an old behavior that formed over a long time with a new one. That takes time.

Don't get caught up in getting it "right now"! The more you do something, the more easily it comes, and over time, you'll start to do it without thinking much about it. And, slow is still progress.

Now not every day will be a perfect progress day. Some days you'll be doing it like a boss. Other days, you'll wonder if you'll even get there. Remember, we learn by trial and error, by doing. It's all ok and even slow progress is progress.

OK, here are a few more tips for reaching your goals:

- Take your time. You didn't learn this behavior over-night. You won't change it overnight.

- Write everything down.

- Use tools that work for you – notebooks, journals, checklists, planners, little rewards - whatever keeps you focused and motivated.

- Expect setbacks. Use them as learning opportunities and be kind to yourself. You're learning.

- Celebrate often. Every step forward is a victory.

Now go set some goals.

Goal	What is your goal? Describe it.

S Specific	What is your goal? Describe it.

M Measurable	What is your goal? Describe it.

A Attainable	What is your goal? Describe it.

R Relevant	What is your goal? Describe it.

T Time Limited	What is your goal? Describe it.

My Smart Goal	What is your goal? Describe it.

STEPS TO SUCCESS LADDER

Use this template to identify your steps to success!

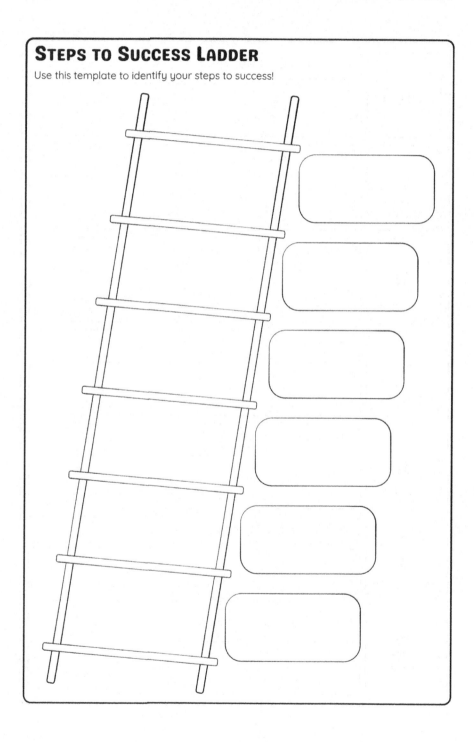

SOCIAL MEDIA AGREEMENT

This agreement is between me _____ and my parents _____ and _____ to be clear about the way I will use social media.

What I'm Using

I am currently using the following Apps and Services:

- Facebook
- instagram
- TikTok
- Twitter
- WhatsApp
- Netflix
- YouTube
- Snapchat
- Kik
- _____
- _____
- _____

EXPECTATIONS OF USE

1. I will use social media only after my homework and other responsibilities are done.

2. I will put my phone away for the night at _____. My phone will be on the charger in the _____(specify where you will leave your phone).

3. My parents may check my social media use for safety purposes. I agree to share my passwords with them when requested.

4. Parents agree to be respectful of my social media use. They will check it for safe use:

- **Daily** (if there is a safety concern or suspected misuse)
- **Weekly**
- **Bi-Weekly**
- **As Needed**

5. I agree to not create secret social media accounts.

6. I agree to not share personal information that could place me or my family in danger on social media.

7. I agree to use social media responsibly and avoid bullying or dangerous interactions of any kind.

8. Other expectations of parents or of teens (you can both add here)

You: _____   **Date:** _____

Parent: _____   **Date:** _____

3 GOOD THINGS TODAY

1.

2.

3.

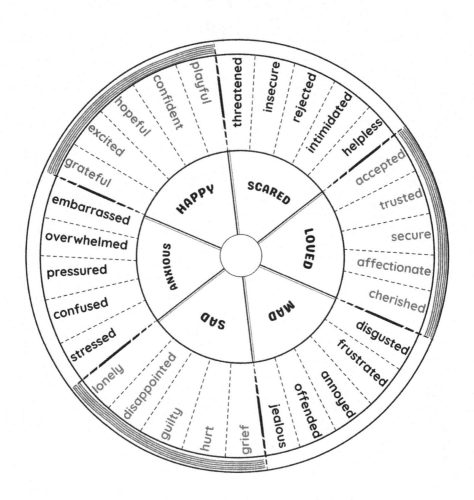

To get the most out of your journaling practice:

1. Pick a journal style that works for you. Maybe you prefer a spiral notebook. Maybe you like those fancy bound journals. You might prefer to journal on your computer or use one of several online journaling options. Choose one that works for your own style.

2. Just write. Don't worry about grammar or style or content. These are your thoughts and your words. There is no right or wrong. Even F bombs. It's your journal and no one sees it unless you choose to share. Allow yourself to fully express yourself in the words you choose.

3. Be consistent. Journaling, like anything else, takes time to become a habit. Set aside a time each day to write.

Trigger/Event	What is the situation that is creating anxiety or distress? Ask: Who? What? Where? When? Who with? How?	
Feelings	0 (no distress) to 10 (extreme distress)	
Automatic/ Negative Thoughts	What are the negative thoughts and images you're having? What do you fear will happen?	
Evidence that supports negative thoughts	What facts do you have that the negative thoughts are true?	
Evidence that does NOT support negative thoughts	What evidence can you find that your negative thoughts are not true? What do others say about the situation?	
Coping Alternatives	What advice would you give your best friend? Is there another way of seeing the situation? What could you do differently? What would be more effective? What does your best, most realistic outcome look like?	
Re-rate Feelings/ Sensations	0 (no distress) to 10 (extreme distress) Imagine your best action to most likely outcome	

EXTRA BONUS

Want to Raise Resilient, Confident, and Future-Ready Teens?

SCAN ME

Parenting teens comes with its own set of challenges, but you don't have to navigate it alone. We've created **The Complete Checklist for Raising Resilient, Confident, and Future-Ready Teens**—a practical guide filled with actionable tips from parenting experts, counselors, and teachers to help you support your teen's growth and success.

https://www.raiseyouthright.com/c/checklist

Resources

Chapter 1: Who Are You?

Personality | Definition, types, nature, & facts. (n.d.). Encyclopedia Britannica. https://www.britannica.com/topic/personality

Dumont, F. (2010). *A history of personality psychology: Theory, science, and research from hellenism to the twenty-first century*. Cambridge University Press.

Myers-Briggs. (2019, November 25). Psychology Today. https://www.psychologytoday.com/us/basics/myers-briggs

Big 5 personality traits. (2017, November 22). Psychology Today. https://www.psychologytoday.com/us/basics/big-5-personality-traits

Roberts, B. W., & DelVecchio, W. F. (2000). The rank-order consistency of personality traits from childhood to old age: a quantitative review of longitudinal studies. *Psychological bulletin*, *126*(1), 3–25. https://doi.org/10.1037/0033-2909.126.1.3

Borghuis, J., Denissen, J., Oberski, D., Sijtsma, K., Meeus, W., Branje, S., Koot, H. M., & Bleidorn, W. (2017). Big Five personality stability, change, and codevelopment across adolescence and early adulthood. *Journal of personality and social psychology*, *113*(4), 641–657. https://doi.org/10.1037/pspp0000138

Giedd J. N. (2008). The teen brain: insights from neuroimaging. *The Journal of adolescent health : official publication of the Society for*

Adolescent Medicine, 42(4), 335–343. https://doi.org/10.1016/j.jadohealth.2008.01.007

Chapter 2: Self Esteem, Confidence, And Being Your Best Self

Mayo Clinic. (2020, July 14). *Self-esteem Grown-ups esteem grows Low or Just Right?* https://www.mayoclinic.org/healthy-lifestyle/adult-health/in-depth/self-esteem/art-20047976

James Ridgway, A. (2009). The inner voice. *International Journal of English Studies*, 9(2). Retrieved from https://revistas.um.es/ijes/article/view/90741

Peters, U. (2020). What is the function of confirmation bias? *Erkenntnis*. https://doi.org/10.1007/s10670-020-00252-1

Abdel-Khalek, A. M. (2016). INTRODUCTION TO THE PSYCHOLOGY OF SELF-ESTEEM. In *Self-esteem: perspectives, influences, and improvement strategies* (pp. 1-23). Nova Science Publisher. https://www.researchgate.net/publication/311440256_Introduction_to_the_Psychology_of_self-esteem

Chapter 3: Communication

Merriam-Webster. (n.d.). *Definition of communication*. Dictionary by Merriam-Webster: America's most-trusted online dictionary. https://www.merriam-webster.com/dictionary/communication

Akilandeswari, V., Dinesh Kumar, A., Philomin Freeda, A., & Niranchan Kumar, S. (2015). Elements of Effective Communication. *New Media and Mass Communication*, 37. https://www.iiste.org/

Topornycky, J., & Golparian, S. (2016). Balancing openness and interpretation in active listening. *Collected Essays on Learning and Teaching*, 9, 175. https://files.eric.ed.gov/fulltext/EJ1104498.pdf

Segal, J., Smith, M., Boose, G., & Jaffe, J. (2015). Nonverbal Communication. Retrieved from http://www.helpguide.org/articles/relationships/nonverbal-communication.htm.

Chapter 4: Navigating Social Media

Social media and teens. (n.d.). Retrieved from https://www.aacap.org/AACAP/Families_and_Youth/Facts_for_Families/FFF-Guide/Social-Media-and-Teens-100.aspx

Pew Research Center. (2019, December 31). 1. Teens and their experiences on social media. Retrieved from https://www.pewresearch.org/internet/2018/11/28/teens-and-their-experiences-on-social-media/

American Academy of Pediatrics https://www.healthychildren.org/English/news/Pages/Managing-Media-We-Need-a-Plan.aspx

Chapter 5: Managing Social Anxiety

National Institute of Mental Health. (n.d.). Anxiety Disorder. Retrieved from https://www.nimh.nih.gov/health/statistics/any-anxiety-disorder

The American Institute of Stress. (2017, January 4). *Take a deep breath.* https://www.stress.org/take-a-deep-breath

Fletcher, J. (2019, February 12). *4-7-8 breathing: How it works, benefits, and uses.* Medical and health information. https://www.medicalnewstoday.com/articles/324417

Box breathing benefits and techniques. (2021, August 16). Cleveland Clinic. https://health.clevelandclinic.org/box-breathing-benefits/

Chorpita, B. F., Taylor, A. A., Francis, S. E., Moffitt, C., & Austin, A. A. (2004). Efficacy of modular cognitive behavior therapy for childhood anxiety disorders. *Behavior Therapy*, 35(2), 263-287. https://doi.org/10.1016/s0005-7894(04)80039-x

Chapter 6: We Have A Situation

Gloria Willcox (1982) The Feeling Wheel, Transactional Analysis Journal, 12:4, 274-276, DOI: 10.1177/036215378201200411

Novella, J. K., Ng, K., & Samuolis, J. (2020). A comparison of online and in-person counseling outcomes using solution-focused brief therapy for college students with anxiety. *Journal of American College Health*, 1-8. https://doi.org/10.1080/07448481.2020.1786101

Chapter 7: Manage Your Stress Before It Manages You

Merriam-Webster Dictionary. (n.d.). Definition of stress. Retrieved from https://www.merriam-webster.com/dictionary/stress

Romeo R. D. (2013). The Teenage Brain: The Stress Response and the Adolescent Brain. *Current directions in psychological science*, 22(2), 140–145. https://doi.org/10.1177/0963721413475445

M. K. Anniko, K. Boersma & M. Tillfors (2019) Sources of stress and worry in the development of stress-related mental health problems: A longitudinal investigation from early- to mid-adolescence, *Anxiety, Stress & Coping*, 32:2, 155-167, DOI: 10.1080/10615806.2018.1549657

American Psychological Association. (2018, October). Stress in American: Generation Z. Retrieved from https://www.apa.org/news/press/releases/stress/2018/stress-gen-z.pdf

Twenge, J. M., Cooper, A. B., Joiner, T. E., Duffy, M. E., & Binau, S. G. (2019). Age, period, and cohort trends in mood disorder indicators and suicide-related outcomes in a nationally representative dataset, 2005-2017. *Journal of abnormal psychology*, 128(3), 185–199. https://doi.org/10.1037/abn0000410

Merriam-Webster. (n.d.). Mindfulness. In *Merriam-Webster.com dictionary*. Retrieved October 31, 2021, from https://www.merriam-webster.com/dictionary/mindfulness

Killingsworth, M. A., & Gilbert, D. T. (2010). A wandering mind is an unhappy mind. *Science, 330*(6006), 932-932. https://doi.org/10.1126/science.1192439

Davis, D. M., & Hayes, J. A. (2012, July). *What are the benefits of mindfulness?* https://www.apa.org. https://www.apa.org/monitor/2012/07-08/ce-corner

Allison Utley & Yvonne Garza (2011) The Therapeutic Use of Journaling With Adolescents, Journal of Creativity in Mental Health, 6:1, 29-41, DOI: 10.1080/15401383.2011.557312

Wood, A. M., Froh, J. J., & Geraghty, A. W. (2010). Gratitude and well-being: A review and theoretical integration. *Clinical Psychology Review, 30*(7), 890-905. https://doi.org/10.1016/j.cpr.2010.03.005

Addendum for Parents

Miller, J. M., DiIorio, C., & Dudley, W. (2002). Parenting style and adolescent's reaction to conflict: Is there a relationship? *Journal of Adolescent Health, 31*(6), 463-468. https://doi.org/10.1016/s1054-139x(02)00452-4

Frijns, T., Finkenauer, C., & Keijsers, L. (2013). Shared secrets versus secrets kept private are linked to better adolescent adjustment. *Journal of Adolescence, 36*(1), 55-64. https://doi.org/10.1016/j.adolescence.2012.09.005

Made in the USA
Coppell, TX
18 May 2025

49543671R00115